TEXT BY A. WILSON GREENE

Maps by George Skoch

Thanks to Chris Bryce, Ray Brown, Ed Raus, and the interpretive staff at Manassas National Battlefield Park.

Published by Eastern National, copyright 2002.

Eastern National provides quality educational products and services to
America's national parks and other public trusts.

Cover: I Will Be Moving Within the Hour, by Mort Künstler. Copyright 1993, Mort Künstler Incorporated.

Back cover: The Diehards, by Don Troiani. Photograph courtesy of Historical Art Prints, Ltd., Southbury, Connecticut.

Printed on recycled paper.

The Second Battle of Manassas

On September 8, 1862, Michigan general Alpheus S. Williams wrote home about the recently concluded military events in northern Virginia. Williams's descriptive language left no doubt that the results had been unfavorable to the Union cause: "a splendid army almost demoralized, millions of public property given up or destroyed, thousands of lives of our best men sacrificed for no purpose." And with equal clarity, Williams identified the source of the debacle: "I dare not trust myself to speak of this commander as I feel and believe. Suffice it to say . . . that more insolence, superciliousness, ignorance, and pretentiousness were never combined in one man."

That man was John Pope, and the failed campaign over which he presided has tarnished Pope's reputation for more than 130 years. Known in the North as Second Bull Run and in the South as Second Manassas, the actions between August 16 and September 2, 1862, marked the midpoint of a momentous season that lifted the Confederacy's fortunes from the brink of disaster to near independence. The gray-clad architects of this achievement, Robert E. Lee and Thomas J. "Stonewall" Jackson, would earn widespread renown from their victory at Second Manassas while Pope vanished into the backwater of history, confused about the cause of his defeat until his dying day.

John Pope (LC)

At the outset of the Civil War's second summer, the Union's prospects appeared bright. Federal armies in the West had penetrated into northern Mississippi and Alabama, New Orleans had fallen, and the navy threatened to reduce Vicksburg and reopen the Mississippi River. Along the Atlantic coast, Yankee forces had captured strong points in the Carolinas, and the primary Northern weapon, the Army of the Potomac under its charismatic but cautious leader George B. McClellan, bivouacked within seven miles of the Confederate capital at Richmond, Virginia.

The principal disappointment amid this sea of encouragement occurred in Virginia's Shenandoah Valley during May and June. An outnumbered aggregration of Confederates under Stonewall Jackson had dispatched portions of three Union commands and then slipped east to reinforce Lee around Richmond. President Abraham Lincoln recognized that Jackson owed much of his success to the fragmented nature of his Federal opponents. On June 26 Lincoln rectified this problem by creating a unified command out of the wreckage of Jackson's Valley victims, styling the new outfit the Army of Virginia. To lead this force the president selected a forty-year-old West Pointer born in Kentucky and raised in Illinois who brought to the job an impressive portfolio.

John Pope combined family connec-

With an outnumbered Confederate army, "Stonewall" Jackson embarrassed portions of three Union armies in the Shenandoah Valley.

(LC)

tions, military experience, and the right politics to merit his appointment. He could trace his roots to George Washington, but more important, the general's father had served as an Illinois circuit judge and knew Lincoln well. Pope's father-in-law represented an Ohio district in Congress and maintained a close relationship with cabinet member Salmon P. Chase. Mrs. Lincoln's eldest sister had married a Pope, so it was not surprising that in 1861 the young officer accompanied the president-elect to Washington for the inauguration.

Pope's prewar military career included competent service in Mexico and on the frontier. He received a commission as brigadier general of volunteers in 1861 and demonstrated his skill with a series of minor victories in the West. Pope owed his promotion and transfer east, however, more to his politics than to his military acumen. The Lincoln administration had grown weary of McClellan's conservative approach to the war, a philosophy embraced by the Democratic party and dedicated to the restoration of the Union with minimal damage to the Southern fabric of life. Pope had Republican leanings, radical ones at that, and he offered the administration a counterpoint to the popular McClellan.

While there were those in the army who spoke highly of Pope, by and large his fellow officers considered him vain, self-righteous, and obnoxious. Various colleagues commented upon his quick temper and rudeness in manner and characterized him as a braggart and liar. "We looked forward with keen delight to see this inflated gas bag punctured by the keen rapier of

Robert E. Lee

(LC)

our great commander," chuckled one Confederate.

Pope exacerbated his unenviable notoriety with a series of orders issued shortly after his arrival in Virginia. Three of them reflected the administration's desire to wage a harder war against the rebellious population. They permitted appropriation of civilian property providing reimbursement only to loyal citizens, authorized stiff penalites for guerrilla activities, and required military-aged males within Union lines to take a loyalty oath or be expelled beyond the limits of Federal control. These measures, although only sporadically enforced and mild by late-war standards, secured Pope the particular opprobrium of most Confederates, including Robert E. Lee, who styled him a "miscreant."

Pope intended to inspire his troops with a formula for victory. "Success and glory are in the advance, disaster and shame lurk in the rear," he exhorted his men.

Equally significant would be his proclamation of July 14 addressed to the "Officers and Soldiers of the Army of Virginia" in which Pope intended to inspire his troops with a formula for victory. "Success and glory are in the advance, disaster and shame lurk in the rear," he exhorted his men. Pope's rallying cry found favor with many of the rank and file but rubbed the officer corps, who felt targeted by their new commander's criticisms, the wrong way. It especially infuriated McClellan and the Army of the Potomac, a result neither unintended nor unanticipated by the administration. Pope's insistence that his new army discard overconcern about lines of supply and possible retreat routes (hallmarks of McClellan's timid generalship) would possess a humiliating irony at the campaign's conclusion.

While Pope spent the first month of his tenure ruffling feathers from Washington, his three leading subordinates assumed responsibility for activities in the field. The German-American idol, Franz Sigel, led Pope's First Corps. Sigel had replaced the dashing but modestly gifted John C. Fremont, who refused to serve under Pope. Sigel's qualifications for command rested with his ethnicity rather than his martial prowess. One Federal officer aptly described him as "altogether excitable, helter-skelter, and unreliable as a military leader."

Nathaniel P. Banks commanded the Second Corps, previously known as the Department of the Shenandoah. This prominent Massachusetts politician had served as Speaker of the House of Representatives and left the statehouse in Boston to accept an appointment as major general of volunteers. Jackson had dominated the hapless Banks during the Valley Campaign earning the New Englander ridicule beyond even what his incompetency deserved. One observer noted that had Banks entered the service as a line officer

FRANZ SIGEL

(USAMHI)

NATHANIEL BANKS

(USAMHI)

under a strict colonel, "he would, probably, eventually, have become a good regimental commander."

Pope's favorite underling led the Third Corps, although Irvin McDowell enjoyed far less popularity among his men than did Sigel or Banks. McDowell graduated from the United States Military Academy and following a respectable prewar career presided over the Union defeat at First Manassas in July 1861. This unfortunate legacy translated into groundless rumors of McDowell's alleged duplicity, symbolized by a ridiculous straw hat which some soldiers considered to be a signal to protect him from Confederate fire. False reports about McDowell's excessive drinking combined with factual depictions of the general's gargantuan appetite to paint an unflattering and uninspiring portrait.

Poor leadership compromised the army's enthusiasm that summer, but so did the discouraging strategic circumstances confronting Pope. His original mission included protecting Washington and the Shenandoah Valley, operating against the Virginia Central Railroad, and, in concert with McClellan's offensive, threatening Richmond from the west. By July 2, however, Lee had driven McClellan from the Confederate capital during the Seven Days' Battles, and a month later the Army of the Potomac received orders to board ships and return to northern Virginia to unite with Pope. Thus Pope faced the challenge of opposing any Confederate push to the north until McClellan's men could arrive, preferably via Fredericksburg and up the line of the Rappahannock River. Achieving all these goals with a dispirited army of barely 55,000 troops presented Pope and his men with a daunting assignment.

DURING THE SEVEN DAYS' BATTLES, LEE TURNED BACK MCCLELLAN FROM THE GATES OF RICHMOND.

(LC)

Robert E. Lee and the Army of Northern Virginia well understood the strategic situation and its potential rewards. The fifty-five-year-old Virginian had assembled a collection of disparate commands to defeat McClellan during the Seven Days and in July detached three divisions under Stonewall Jackson to keep an eye on Pope. As long as McClellan remained with-

At the Battle of Cedar Mountain on August 9, Jackson earned a hard-won victory over Nathaniel Banks.

(LC)

Thomas J. "Stonewall" Jackson

(LC)

in striking distance of Richmond, however, Lee could not afford to deprive the capital of its mobile defenses.

Early in August, Lee had accumulated a variety of evidence that foretold the departure of the Army of the Potomac from its position below Richmond. Then on August 9 Jackson thrashed Banks in a convincing if imperfectly fought engagement at Cedar Mountain north of the Rapidan River, intimidating Pope and seizing the initiative from the Federals.

McClellan's imminent flight and Banks's defeat offered Lee the opportunity he coveted. He ordered the right wing of his army under James Longstreet (the Confederate government had not yet authorized the formation of corps) to march northwest and join Jackson near Gordonsville, a vital rail junction linking Richmond with the Shenandoah Valley and northern Virginia. Lee's job would be to "suppress" Pope before McClellan could reinforce him.

Jackson and Longstreet brought some 55,000 soldiers to the task, most of them veterans of the victories around Richmond, and Lee's lieutenants suffered from none of the shortcomings that handicapped Pope's corps commanders. James Longstreet, a classmate of Pope's at West Point, was a forty-two-year-old transplanted Georgian. He distinguished himself as Lee's most effective subordinate during the Seven Days and would remain a trusted, if occasionally controversial, member of Lee's inner circle throughout the entire war. Jackson's fame exceeded Lee's at this stage in history. The Virginian's reputation earned at First Manassas and in the Valley made him the most admired (and feared) figure in Confederate gray.

Indeed, it was Stonewall who urged Lee that the united Rebel army should strike Pope immediately. Two small divisions under Jesse L. Reno, a portion of Ambrose E. Burnside's North Carolina command, had already arrived via Fredericksburg augmenting Pope's strength along the Rapidan. If the Confederates moved quickly against the Federal left flank, they could sever the reinforcement pipeline from Fredericksburg and catch

Pope's whole army with the Rappahannock River at its back, possibly crushing it in the process.

Lee agreed but opted to delay the attack until Southern cavalry under his nephew, Fitzhugh Lee, could execute a raid to destroy the Orange & Alexandria Railroad bridge across the Rappahannock in Pope's rear. By August 17 both Longstreet and Jackson poised in concealed positions south of the Rapidan waiting for Fitz Lee and the signal to launch the offensive scheduled for the next day.

Unfortunately for the Confederates, no one had told the young cavalryman that Lee's plan depended upon his prompt appearance. Fitz Lee tarried en route to collect supplies, forcing his uncle Robert to postpone the advance. Even these revised plans came to grief when on the night of the seventeenth a mounted Union patrol splashed across an unguarded ford on the Rapidan and surprised Confederate cavalry chieftain J.E.B. Stuart at his headquarters early the next morning. Stuart barely made good an escape which cost him his cape, a new plumed hat, and a great deal of pride. One of Stuart's aides did fall captive to the Union intruders, surrendering two satchels of dispatches he carried containing Lee's orders for Pope's undoing.

Thus warned of his impending demise, Pope began a hasty withdrawal to the Rappahannock, crossing that watery barrier on the night of the nineteenth to twentieth. "We little thought that the enemy would turn his back upon us this early in the campaign," Lee told Longstreet in a feeble attempt to joke about the disappointing turn of events. The Confederates pursued, many of them fording the Rapidan "guiltless of any clothing below the waist" but could not prevent Pope from placing the Rappahannock between them and their quarry. The Federals thus scored the first strategic point of the new campaign.

As the armies glared at one another from opposite banks of the Rappahannock, each commander confronted a quandary. Pope had to provide a secure corridor for

J.E.B. STUART

(LC)

reinforcements from the Army of the Potomac. Those fresh troops might arrive from Fredericksburg, requiring Pope to protect his left flank downstream on the Rappahannock. McClellan's units could also disembark on the Potomac at Alexandria and employ Pope's direct supply line, the Orange & Alexandria Railroad, to reach the front. Pope knew that this avenue might be breached by skirting his right flank and gaining his rear, necessitating Federal vigilance along the upper Rappahannock. The man in charge of coordinating the rendezvous between Pope and McClellan, General in Chief Henry W. Halleck, found his task overwhelming and provided Pope little guidance. Halleck did encourage McClellan to hasten the move-

Railroad bridge on the Orange & Alexandria line.

(USAMHI)

ment of his army to northern Virginia, but "Little Mac" pursued his assignment with glacial speed, a function both of his natural inclination and his loathing for the arrogant Pope.

Lee's dilemma centered on the realization that he must find a way to engage the Federals. But forcing a downstream crossing of the Rappahannock would expose his army to an attack from the direction of Fredericksburg while shortening the distance that Union reinforcements must cover to reach Pope. Thus the Confederate commander looked upstream to the north and west to find the means of outwitting Pope's defenders.

On August 21 a small body of Southerners slipped across the river at Beverly Ford, but the Federals reacted quickly and Lee recalled his men. The north side of the Rappahannock physically dominated the south bank, and Pope skillfully exploited his geographic advantage. Consequently, Lee shifted even farther upriver, authorizing Jackson to cross at Sulphur Springs, nine miles above Beverly Ford, and approving "Jeb" Stuart's suggestion to conduct a cavalry raid behind Pope's lines.

On August 22 Jackson managed to maneuver a reinforced brigade with a battery of artillery across the river before dark. Heavy downpours that night swelled the Rappahannock beyond fording stage, however, and Jackson worked furiously the next day to reestablish contact with his isolated and vulnerable units.

Meanwhile Stuart led some 1,500 troopers on a daring ride around Pope's right, descending after dark on Catlett Station along the Orange & Alexandria Railroad. Not only did Catlett provide a home for most of Pope's headquarters impedimentia, but the railroad bridge over nearby Cedar Run offered a tempting target for Stuart's raiders. If the Confederates could destroy that span, Pope's supply line would be broken and, perhaps, the Federals would be compelled to relinquish their tenacious grip along the Rappahannock.

One of the marauders remembered

On the night of August 22, Stuart led a daring raid on Pope's headquarters located at Catlett Station.

(LC)

that at 7:30 P.M., in the midst of a torrential thunderstorm, "the bugles rang out . . . half a note of the stirring call—the rest was drowned by a roar like Niagara. From two thousand throats came the dreaded [Rebel] yell, and at full gallop two thousand horsemen came thundering on." The attack caught the rear-echelon headquarters staff and their small infantry guard by complete surprise. "The cavalry rode among the tents and their shock knocked some of the officers out of bed," said one Union observer. "Every man, white and black, high and low, fled on his own hook." While some of Stuart's despoilers pillaged the well-stocked encampment, others attempted in vain to set fire to the saturated bridge over Cedar Run. After midnight Stuart rounded up his high-spirited horsemen and headed back for safe crossings on the upper Rappahannock.

Stuart's failure to destroy the railroad bridge robbed the Catlett raid of its primary strategic potential. The beau sabruer did, however, assauge his bruised ego by avenging the loss of his plumed hat. Among the prizes gathered at Pope's headquarters tent was the Union general's full-dress uniform coat. Stuart wrote Pope suggesting "a cartel for the fair exchange of the prisoners," to which he received no response. As a result, Stuart had Pope's splendid garment displayed in the picture window of a Richmond store and elsewhere in the Confederate capital, where it attracted crowds of "amused spectators."

More meaningfully, Stuart showed Lee captured correspondence verifying the rapid approach of McClellan's men from both Fredericksburg and Alexandria. In fact, John F. Reynolds's division had already reached Kelly's Ford on the Rappahannock while the rest of Fitz John Porter's Fifth Corps marched a day behind. Samuel P. Heintzelman's Third Corps had landed in Alexandria and awaited transportation to the front. Clearly the window for Lee to strike at Pope under numerically favorable circumstances was closing fast.

On August 24, Lee issued orders that would send Jackson and his 24,000 men on their march around Pope's army.

(*I Will Be Moving Within the Hour* by Mort Künstler, copyright 1993.)

On August 23 the Confederates faced the more immediate problem of extricating Jackson's men from the north bank of the river near Sulphur Springs. While Sigel slowly descended on the unsupported graycoats, Jackson completed the construction of a new bridge late in the day and removed his relieved troops before dawn on the twenty-fourth. But within twenty-four hours Jackson would have them back across the Rappahannock, this time in much greater strength.

JACKSON'S FLANK MARCH, AUGUST 25–27, 1862
In the early morning hours of August 25, Jackson's men began crossing the Rappahannock River at Hinson's Mill Ford. Forty-eight hours later after covering fifty-six miles in the blistering August heat, Jackson lighted in the rear of Pope's army at Manassas Junction.

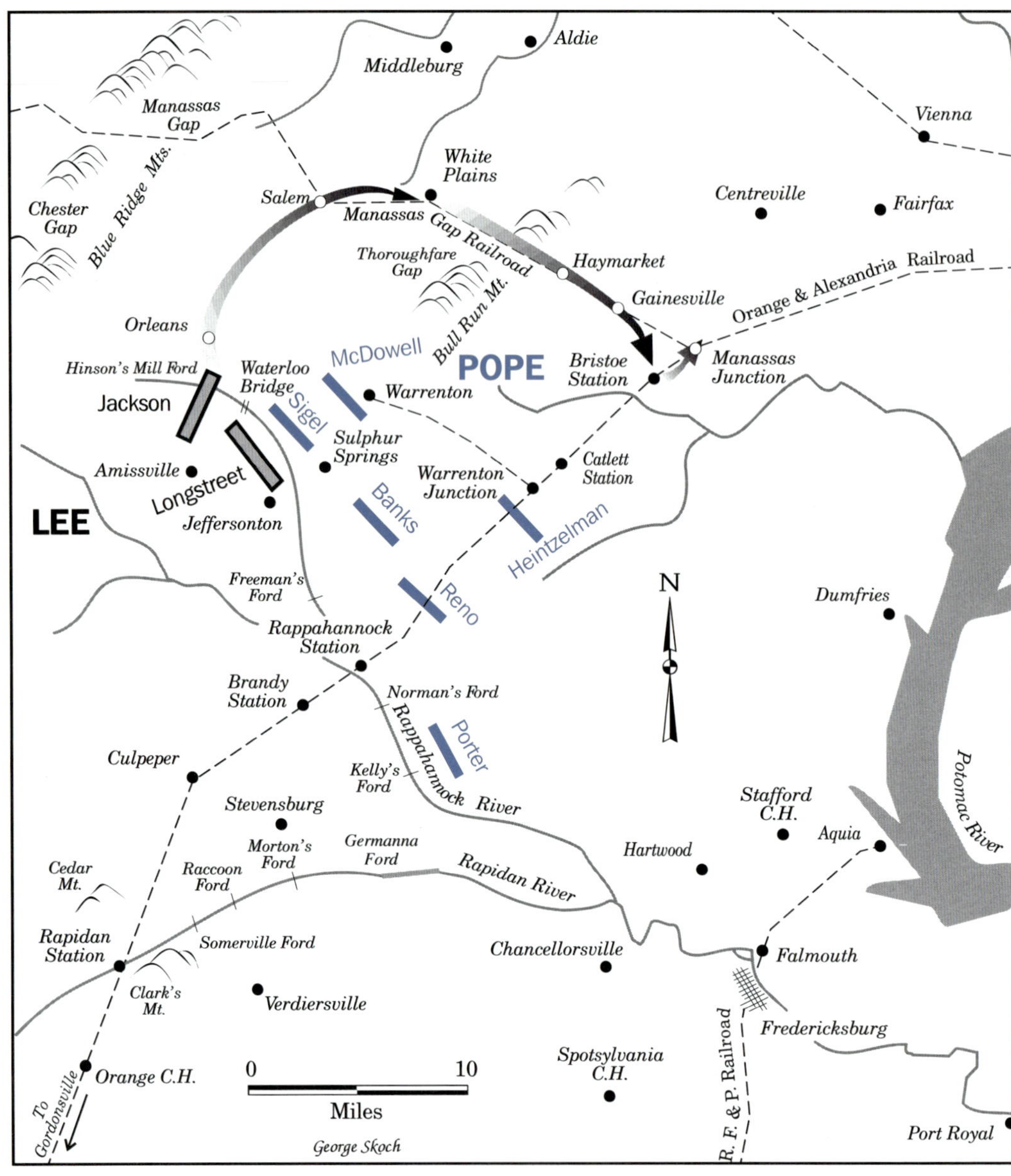

No matter what the potential rewards, Lee's scheme involved great risk.

This movement would result from a council of war conducted on August 24 by General Lee at the village of Jeffersonton. The white-bearded commander explained his intention to send Jackson's entire wing, some 24,000 men, on an ambitious march around Pope's right flank to alight somewhere in the Union rear. Building upon the concept tested by Stuart at Catlett Station, Jackson's force would fracture Pope's supply line and thus persuade the Yankees to retire from their Rappahannock defenses. From there the Army of Northern Virginia would respond to whatever strategic opportunities the situation presented, including a chance to strike Pope with advantage or a possible movement into Maryland.

No matter what the potential rewards, Lee's scheme involved great risk. Longstreet's divisions would occupy Pope's attention along the Rappahannock during Jackson's flank march, but the wings of the Confederate army would be dangerously divided. Should Pope discover Jackson's detachment before Longstreet could close the gap, half of the Confederate infantry faced mortal peril. Moreover, Lee knew that every day might bring fresh units of McClellan's men to the equation. Confederate strategy at Second Manassas thus rivaled the audacity of any grand plan of the Civil War.

Lee accepted the gamble because of his confidence in Stonewall Jackson. "Old Blue Light" relished assignments such as this and used his experience in the Shenandoah Valley as a model. Early on the morning of August 25 Jackson assembled his three divisions, issued orders for an expeditious, disciplined march, and began a journey that would take his troops twenty-five miles before day's end.

Richard S. Ewell's brigades led the way. Ewell served under Jackson in the Valley, and the two Virginians had established a relationship of trust and mutual respect. Jackson's largest division, that of Ambrose Powell Hill, followed Ewell. Hill possessed substantial military talent leavened with a fiery temper and an oversensitivity to criticism and had already run afoul of his infamously unforgiving commander. Jackson's old division, now under William B. Taliaferro, brought up the rear. Jackson thought little of Taliaferro and by year's end would rid himself of a man he considered unreliable. The column waded a branch of the Rappahannock, tramped across fields, and negotiated streams heedless of any specific highway. Their northward orientation led them to a point near Salem (present-day Marshall), where the weary Confederates fell to earth for a short night's rest.

A movement of this magnitude could not go unnoticed. Indeed, early in the morning alert Federal signal stations spotted Jackson's column, and before noon Pope obtained an accurate idea about its size and direction. What the Yankee observers could not decipher was Jackson's ultimate destination, and here Pope stumbled. Instead of retiring from the Rappahannock to block Jackson's approach, protect his supply base at Manassas Junction, and prepare to unite with McClellan's units moving south from Alexandria, Pope concluded that the Confederates were shifting away from him toward the Shenandoah Valley.

JACKSON'S "FOOT CAVALRY" ON THE MARCH.

(*BL*)

Pope's error allowed Jackson on August 26 to turn east and pass without interference through Thoroughfare Gap, a narrow defile in the Bull Run Mountains. This craggy range of hills presented the only natural obstacle between Jackson and the railroad. Likewise, safe passage through Thoroughfare Gap provided the key to Longstreet's eventual rendezvous with Stonewall somewhere on the plains of Manassas. "Old Pete" had done his job well and left the Rappahannock late that afternoon, but by then Jackson had covered more than fifty miles in the thirty-four

AFTER MARCHING IN THE STIFLING SUMMER HEAT, JACKSON'S EXHAUSTED SOLDIERS DINED ON WHAT LITTLE THEY COULD FORAGE FROM THE SURROUNDING FIELDS.

(*BL*)

One after the other, the locomotives careened off the broken and barricaded rails creating a spectacular scene of destruction. Had the cars been loaded with soldiers, Jackson's men would have captured or killed them all.

hours since his departure. "The march had been a rapid one and the soldiers were weary, faint, and footsore," admitted one participant, but all the labors of the past two days would mean nothing unless Stonewall could take advantage of his perilous position in Pope's rear earned by the exertion of his legendary "foot cavalry."

Pope's supply depot at Manassas Junction, the uninhabited intersection of the Orange & Alexandria and Manassas Gap railroads, offered the greatest reward to Jackson's exhausted brigades. But Stonewall opted to steer his men first toward Bristoe Station, a whistle stop several miles southwest of the junction. Seizing Bristoe and wrecking the nearby bridge over Broad Run would cut Pope's direct rail connection with his base and place a free-flowing obstacle between Manassas and its dependent Union army. Moreover, Jackson learned that only a handful of Federals guarded Bristoe, and he speculated that Manassas might be better protected.

Early in the evening Stonewall's cavalry escort swooped upon the startled Pennsylvanians carelessly encamped around Bristoe, dispersing them with ease. Just then a whistle blast alerted the Confederates to the approach of an empty Federal supply train returning to Manassas from the front. Although the gray-clad raiders attempted to block the tracks, the engineer barreled through occupied Bristoe, eventually spreading the word that a Confederate force had once again gained Pope's rear. But his warning did not reach the next two trainmen, who fell victim to Jackson's vandals. One after the other, the locomotives careened off the broken and barricaded rails creating a spectacular scene of destruction. Had the cars been loaded with soldiers, Jackson's men would have captured or killed them all.

The only Yankees in the neighborhood, however, were four miles up the tracks at Manassas. The junction's small garrison responded to the engineer's alarm by deploying infantry and artillery who prepared to resist what they believed to be another cavalry raid similar to Stuart's foray against Catlett.

Despite the late hour and the dusty miles already logged that day, sixty-year-old Isaac R. Trimble volunteered two of his regiments for the task of capturing Manassas. Supported by some of Stuart's cavalry, Trimble pounced on the overmatched Unionists about midnight. "Our

CONFEDERATE SUPPLY WAGONS NEGOTIATE A WATER CROSSING DURING THE FLANK MARCH.

(LC)

boys gave them our best, but they were so close that our artillery only got in about two or three shots apiece, when, in overwhelming numbers, they were right among us in the darkness," reported the Federal commander. Most of the Unionists surrendered. Jackson had thus brilliantly accomplished the first portion of his assignment, but his ultimate achievement would depend on the Federals' reaction.

To his credit, Pope saw opportunity where others might have panicked. The Federal commander reasoned that an undetermined fraction of Lee's army had advanced beyond its immediate supports, offering a rare opportunity to crush his enemy in detail. Pope directed his 66,000 men along the Rappahannock to abandon their positions on August 27 and fan out along an eight-mile arc between the Warrenton-Alexandria Turnpike on the left and the Orange & Alexandria Railroad on the right. McDowell, in command of his own and Sigel's corps, would take the turnpike, Reno and Philip Kearny's division of Heintzelman's corps would occupy the center, while Heintzelman's other division under "Fighting Joe" Hooker, followed by Porter's corps, would tramp beside the tracks toward Bristoe and Manassas. Banks, still recovering from Cedar Mountain, would guard the army's wagons in the rear.

Thirty miles east of Manassas Junction, General Halleck responded to what on the night of August 26–27 he assumed to be only a cavalry incursion. With the assistance of the energetic chief of military railroads, Herman Haupt, Halleck assembled a reinforced brigade under George W. Taylor to move toward Manassas, expel the pesky raiders, and reestablish rail communication with Pope. Halleck also instructed McClellan's newly arrived Sixth Corps under William B. Franklin to march toward Gainesville on the Warrenton Turnpike and unite with Pope's expanding army. Pope and Halleck, incommunicado because Jackson had clipped the telegraph wires between Washington and the Rappahannock, had thus unknowingly orchestrated a potent envelopment of Jackson's isolated wing. Some 80,000 Federals were converging on Manassas from opposite directions, and if all went well, Stonewall and his three divisions might be eliminated.

As the sun rose on August 27, how-

ORDERED TO MAINTAIN SILENCE, JACKSON'S MEN RAISE THEIR HATS IN MUTE TRIBUTE TO THEIR BELOVED COMMANDER.

(*OLD JACK* BY DON TROIANI, COURTESY OF HISTORICAL ART PRINTS LTD., SOUTHBURY, CONNECTICUT)

Confederate troops pillaging Manassas Junction likened it to a "Warehouse filled with all the delicacies."

(BL)

Jackson's men burned what they could not carry, leaving the Federal supply depot a smoldering ruin.

(LC)

ever, Jackson's first concern was to reinforce Trimble at Manassas Junction. Stonewall left Ewell at Bristoe to protect the Confederate rear and marched with Hill and Taliaferro to the Union supply base. The sight that greeted the ragged Confederate scarecrows boggled their minds. "At the Junction was a large depot of stores [and] two trains containing probably two hundred large cars loaded down with many millions of quartermaster and commissary stores," gushed one Rebel. "Beside these, there were very large sutlers' depots, full of everything. In short, there was collected there, in the space of a square mile, an amount and variety of property such as I had never conceived of."

Before the awestruck Southerners had a fair chance to sample this inspiring cornucopia, Jackson's pickets announced the appearance of enemy troops. Hill's brigades first repulsed a heavy artillery regiment en route to Manassas, but George Taylor's New Jerseyians offered a larger target. The Garden Staters confidently approached to within a few hundred yards of Jackson's concealed defenders before the landscape exploded in a fury of lead and iron. The brave Yankees stood their ground for ten minutes, ignoring Stonewall's personal appeals to surrender. But numbers soon determined the outcome of this lopsided contest, and Taylor retreated precipitately toward Bull Run, losing a third of his men and suffering a mortal wound.

News of Taylor's disaster soon reached Washington, where George McClellan had at last arrived to take command of the Peninsula veterans intended to succor Pope. Instead of hastening Franklin's 10,000 fresh rifles to the front as Halleck intended, McClellan canceled Franklin's advance. "I have no means of knowing the enemy's force between Pope and ourselves," McClellan told the general in chief. "I do not see that we have force enough in hand to form a connection with Pope, whose exact position we do not know." Herman Haupt tried frantically to persuade McClellan of the

Raiding Pope's Pantry

On the evening of August 26, 1862, Jackson reached the Orange & Alexandria Railroad at Bristoe Station, where he and his men derailed two Federal supply trains and destroyed a quarter mile of track. Jackson was soon informed that Manassas Junction, located four miles north of Bristoe, was lightly guarded. The junction was serving as the supply hub for John Pope's army and was said to contain "stores of great value."

Jackson quickly selected two regiments under the command of Issac Trimble to capture the junction. After moving forward, the two regiments quickly seized the depot and 300 prisoners.

Many of the soldiers reflected on the abundant supplies found at Manassas.

"Jackson's first order was to knock out the heads of hundreds of barrels of whiskey, wine, and brandy. I shall never forget the scene. Streams of spirits ran like water through the sands of Manassas and the soldiers on hands and knees drank it greedily from the ground."

Major W. Roy Mason

The Federal depot was "vast storehouses filled with . . . all the delicacies, potted ham, lobster, tongue, candy, cakes, nuts, oranges, lemons, pickles, catsup, mustard, etc. It makes an old soldier's mouth water now just to think of the good things captured there. . . . Some filled their haversacks with cakes, some with candy, others with oranges, lemons, canned goods etc. I know one that took nothing but French mustard . . . it turned out to be the best thing taken because he traded it for meat and bread. It lasted until we reached Frederick."

Private John H. Worsham
21st Virginia Infantry

"I will not attempt to describe the scene I here witnessed for I am sure it beggars description. Just imagine about 6000 men hungry and almost naked, let loose on some million dollars worth of biscuit, cheese, ham, bacon, messpork, coffee, sugar, tea, fruit, brandy, wine, whiskey, oysters, coats, pants, shirts, caps, boots, shoes, socks, blankets, tents, etc.. Here you would see a crowd enter a car with their old confederate grays and in a few moments come out dressed in Yankee uniforms; some as cavalry; some as artillerists; others dressed in the splendid uniform of Federal officers . . . I have often read of the sacking of cities by a victorious army but never did I hear of a railroad train being sacked. I viewed this scene for almost two hours with the most intense anxiety. I saw the whole army become what appeared to me an ungovernable mob."

Chaplain James B. Sheeran
14th Louisiana Infantry

That night, with Pope's army closing in on Manassas Junction, Jackson's men set fire to the remaining supplies. He then moved his men toward the old battlefield of Manassas to await the arrival of Lee and Longstreet.

—Chris Bryce

need and practicality of releasing Franklin, but Little Mac would hear none of it. McClellan had written his wife a few days before that "I don't see how I can remain in the service if placed under Pope," and now his excess caution would ensure that the despised Illinoisan would control no more of the Army of the Potomac until McClellan approved.

Meanwhile, Taylor's defeat allowed Jackson's victorious regiments to indulge in what would possibly be the happiest day of their military lives. "I saw the whole army become what appeared to me an ungovernable mob, drunk, some few with liquor but the others with excitement," remembered a Louisiana chaplain. Actually the pious and prudent Jackson had taken steps to discard the tempting intoxicants stashed among the delicacies stockpiled at Manassas Junction. But the rest of the booty presented fair game for the butternut desperados. The hungry men ate their fill and then stuffed their pockets and haversacks with a variety of edibles, drinkables, and tradables.

Ewell's brigades did not share in the initial revelry because they found less pleasant employment in combat with the vanguard of Pope's army at Bristoe Station. During the afternoon Hooker's division approached the depot from the west and clashed with Ewell for an hour before the Confederates executed a textbook withdrawal. The Rebels crossed Broad Run, firing the bridge in their wake, while the

Before the awestruck Southerners had a fair chance to sample this inspiring cornucopia, Jackson's pickets announced the appearance of enemy troops.

George McClellan

(USAMHI)

bloodied and exhausted Federals licked their wounds at Bristoe. Ewell's men did reach Manassas at dusk and helped themselves to what remained of the Union supplies, but one of Ewell's officers complained that other troops had "appropriated the provisions of a more enticing character."

John Pope indulged in another kind of feast on the night of August 27—an intellectual Bacchanalia featuring the stimulating brew of glorious prospective victory. Learning of Jackson's strength and whereabouts from Hooker's prisoners at Bristoe, Pope made plans "to bag the whole crowd" of brazen Confederates the next day. He eagerly directed his entire army to converge on Manassas Junction from the southwest, west, and north.

Although Pope's conception possessed admirable initiative and aggressiveness, it ignored two fundamental factors. First, Pope's success depended upon the unlikely eventuality that Jackson would quietly remain at Manassas Junction until Pope's scattered divisions could descend upon him from three directions of the compass. Second, he ignored the existence of half of Lee's army, Longstreet's wing, which Pope now knew to be on the march and in the vicinity of Salem. As one of the campaign's early historians wrote a century ago, "the concentration of the entire army on Manassas, ordered as it was on the evening of the 27th . . . . was the parent of much disaster."

Jackson had no intention of remaining stationary at the plundered Union supply base. His strategic imperative depended upon bringing Pope to battle, but only under circumstances favorable to the

When Pope's army arrived at Manassas Junction, Jackson was nowhere to be found.

(LC)

Union soldiers survey the devastated supply depot at Manassas Junction.

(USAMHI)

Confederates. This meant that Lee's army must be reunited, but Jackson's couriers informed him that Longstreet was at least a day's march away. Stonewall would have to purchase that time by adopting a strong position from which he could connect with Longstreet via Thoroughfare Gap. And if they then hoped to attack Pope with advantage, Jackson had to discourage the Union commander from retreating across Bull Run to assume a defensive posture until McClellan joined him with the rest of the Army of the Potomac.

Jackson studied the map and discovered a location that satisfied his criteria perfectly. Stony Ridge, a low rise 1,000 yards north of the Warrenton Turnpike near the old Manassas battlefield, possessed all of Jackson's required virtues. Its heavy woods would conceal the Confederates but allow them a clear view of the highway that might take Pope across Bull Run. Longstreet could link with Jackson there either via the turnpike or a secondary road leading directly from Thoroughfare Gap. Another byway connected Stony Ridge with Aldie Gap in the Bull Run Mountains, offering an escape route for Jackson if Longstreet somehow failed to arrive. Finally, the cuts and fills of an unfinished railroad running along the base of Stony Ridge formed a ready-made entrenchment for Jackson's outnumbered divisions. One thoughtful Confederate considered Jackson's move to Stony Ridge "a masterpiece of strategy, unexcelled during the war."

Taliaferro's division began the march at 9:00 P.M. August 27 along the Manassas-Sudley Road reaching the turnpike near the famous Stone House by midnight. Stonewall intended for Hill and Ewell to follow Taliaferro's lead, but bewildered guides misdirected these troops across Bull Run and in Hill's case all the way to Centreville. It would not be until the next morning that Jackson's entire wing reunited on Stony Ridge. Behind them Manassas Junction lay in charred ruins, a hollow prize for the first Federal troops who appeared there late on the morning of August 28.

In fact, nothing had gone just right for Pope this day. McDowell and Sigel had become ensnarled on the roadways around Gainesville and suffered a five-hour delay in their march toward Manassas. Struggling through tangled terrain, Sigel stumbled

Irvin McDowell

(NA)

cross-country toward Bristoe, each step rendering his corps more irrelevant to the strategic situation. McDowell finally pushed eastward on the turnpike about 10:00 A.M. Reynolds's division of Pennsylvania Reserves led the corps followed by the four brigades of Rufus King. McDowell placed James B. Ricketts's division in the rear with orders to peek over their shoulders toward Thoroughfare Gap, alert to the appearance of Confederates at that critical point. McDowell's precaution proved wise, as events would soon demonstrate.

The four divisions of Longstreet's wing who began their march in Jackson's footsteps on the afternoon of August 26 covered a commendable fourteen miles before sunset, but tramped only six miles on the twenty-seventh. Lee, who traveled with Longstreet, allowed the pace to be equally languid on August 28, a surprising concession considering Jackson's perilous situation on the plains of Manassas. By late morning Longstreet's leading brigades approached the potential chokepoint at Thoroughfare Gap.

McDowell first learned of Longstreet's proximity from one of his overworked cavalry regiments which had been attempting to block the constricted mountain pass with a jumble of felled trees. On his own initiative, McDowell turned Ricketts around and ordered him to use his 5,000 men to plug the bottleneck at Thoroughfare Gap. Ricketts arrived in mid-afternoon and engaged two brigades of Georgians for several bloody hours. Longstreet finally settled the affair by wisely orchestrating a flanking movement on both sides of the gap, offering Ricketts no choice but to retire his outgunned brigades to the east. Longstreet then moved up and secured Thoroughfare Gap, leaving no natural impediment to his unification with Jackson the next day.

Meanwhile, John Pope continued to indulge his fixation with Jackson. The Union commander had snatched a handful of Confederate stragglers at Manassas Junction, who misinformed him that Stonewall had marched just a few hours earlier toward Centreville. Hill and Ewell had, in fact, mistakenly crossed Bull

Battling the Federal soldiers of James Ricketts's division, Longstreet's men forced their way through Thoroughfare Gap.

(LC)

Run the previous night, but by midday August 28 they had rejoined Taliaferro along Stony Ridge. Pope accepted the prisoners' inaccurate intelligence and redirected his army toward Centreville, determined to annihilate Jackson no matter where the wily Confederate might go.

Jackson shared Pope's enthusiam for a fight. His tired but contented men, "packed like herring in a barrel in the woods behind the old railroad," lounged in the August heat awaiting the word to spring on their unwary prey. That word arrived shortly before noon when Reynolds appeared on the turnpike at the head of McDowell's corps just west of Jackson's concealed right flank. Jackson arose "like an electric shock" and ordered Ewell and Taliaferro to move to the attack. But before they could deploy, their quarry had vanished, disappearing down Pageland Lane, a country road that would take the Federals toward Manassas as their current orders demanded. A frustrated Jackson prowled along his lines hoping for another opportunity to strike the Yankees, anxious also to learn about Longstreet's progress.

Toward evening Stonewall received good news on both fronts. A courier reported Longstreet's success at Thoroughfare Gap, suggesting that Old Pete would connect with Jackson's right early the next day. Much relieved, Jackson sought a few moments of rest, indulging in one of his celebrated impromptu naps in the comfort of a fence corner. He had not slumbered long when breathless messengers pounded up and announced the presence of a large column of bluecoats marching eastward on the turnpike across the Confederate front. Jackson mounted in an instant and rode off to see for himself. On the open slope of a pasture belonging to John Brawner's rented farm, northwest of the hamlet of Groveton, Jackson paraded in full view of the passing Federals. The Northerners took little notice of the lone rider whom they assumed to be a mere cavalry scout. Jackson absorbed the scene for a few moments and then returned to his fence-corner headquarters. "Bring out your men, gentlemen," he told his subordinates. The Second Battle of Manassas was about to begin.

Stonewall's Federal targets belonged to Rufus King's division. King, the forty-eight-year-old scion of a distinguished New York family, was McDowell's favorite division commander. Perhaps their warm relationship induced McDowell to overlook his subordinate's failing health. King had suffered an epileptic seizure on August 23 and would experience a recurrence of his malady on the afternoon of the twenty-eighth, leaving him incapable of taking the field during the most critical time in his division's history. Of course, as his four brigades swung east on the turnpike in the waning sunlight, no one could know that the next few hours would prove so consequential.

King's men were responding to orders from Pope received at 5:00 P.M. directing the reconcentration against

CONFEDERATE ARTILLERY POSTED NEAR THE BRAWNER FARM PINNED DOWN THE FEDERAL SOLDIERS OF RUFUS KING'S DIVISION ALONG THE WARRENTON TURNPIKE. (BL)

Centreville. The other divisions of McDowell's corps, Reynolds's and Ricketts's, had proceeded toward Manassas and engaged Longstreet at Thoroughfare Gap respectively, so only King was in position to move immediately toward the new goal. A unique brigade of Westerners led by John Gibbon marched with King's 6,000 men. Gibbon issued his Wisconsin and Indiana soldiers broad-brimmed black hats, lending them a distinctive appearance. Only one of Gibbon's regiments, the Second Wisconsin, had any combat experience under its belt, but the events of August 28 would change all that.

The "black hats" followed John P. Hatch's lead regiments and preceded Abner Doubleday's and Marsena R. Patrick's brigades in King's line of march. "Drowsily we swung along the grassy roadside, taking in the soft beauty of the scene," rhapsodized one of King's soldiers. The terrain around them was mostly open. North of the turnpike, the ground rose gently for 500 yards toward the Brawner house and its adjacent orchard. The unfinished railroad lay 1,000 feet beyond, about one-quarter mile south of the wooded slopes of Stony Ridge. A thirty-acre stand of hickory and oak, Brawner's Woods, straddled the turnpike southeast of the dwelling.

"Our brigade moved along the turnpike on that quiet summer evening as unsuspectingly as if changing camp," remembered an officer in the Sixth Wisconsin. "Suddenly the stillness was broken by six cannon shots fired in rapid succession by a rebel battery, point blank at our regiment." General Gibbon reacted quickly to this unexpected fire by unlimbering his own guns, Battery B, Fourth United States Artillery, which responded to the Confederate shelling coming from the Brawner farm. Additional Southern ordnance entered the fray, the "exchange of metallic compliments [becoming] very profuse indeed."

Jackson's salvos succeeded in halting King's entire division. Hatch had proceeded beyond the focus of the Confederate fire, but Patrick's regiments fled for cover south of the highway while Gibbon's and Doubleday's troops sought shelter in Brawner's woodlot along the road. Those two brigadiers, assuming Jackson to be at Centreville, concluded that this annoyance must be courtesy of Jeb Stuart's horse artillery. Like most infantry commanders, Gibbon had little regard for cavalry in an open fight, so he volunteered to send his veteran Second Wisconsin up the hill to disperse the bothersome cannoneers and their mounted supports.

Company I of the Seventh Wisconsin Volunteers.

(Courtesy State Historical Society of Wisconsin)

The Second Wisconsin, known as "the Ragged Ass Second" because of the condition of their trousers, numbered 430 officers and men. Their colonel, Edgar O'Connor, had lost his voice that day and had to whisper to his adjutant to convey the orders to advance. Shortly after 6:30 P.M. O'Connor directed his troops through Brawner's Woods, emerging in the fields southeast of the farmhouse. The Confederate batteries had already limbered up and pulled away, but on the horizon appeared a long and menacing line of butternut infantry.

These men belonged to the most renowned brigade in Lee's army, the Stonewall Brigade from Virginia's Shenandoah Valley. Earning their blood-stained fame at First Manassas and during the Valley Campaign, Jackson's former command had been reduced to barely 800 bayonets in five regiments. Despite their depleted ranks, a Confederate officer testified that "it made one's blood tingle with pride to see these troops going into action."

O'Connor deployed in line of battle, "the men grasping their pieces with a tighter grip and expressing their impatience in low mutterings in such honest, if not classic phrases, as, 'come on God damn you.'" When the Virginians closed to within 150 yards, the Second Wisconsin let fly a devastating volley. The Confederates shuddered, absorbed the blast, and advanced to an old rail fence 80 yards from their blue-clad opponents, where they at last returned fire. "Everything around us was lighted up by the blaze of the musketry and explosion of balls like a continuous flash of lightning," recalled a Confederate.

Gibbon began to realize that he faced more than a few troublesome troopers. He ordered the "Swamp Hogs" of the Nineteenth Indiana under their six foot-seven inch commander Solomon Meredith to support O'Connor's left. The Hoosiers took position almost in the Brawner front yard, where the Stonewall Brigade greeted them with a punishing sheet of lead.

JOHN GIBBON

(LC)

For some reason, neither Ewell nor Taliaferro moved the rest of their nearby divisions into battle with the alacrity the situation required. A frustrated Jackson found three Georgia regiments belonging to Alexander R. Lawton's brigade and personally led them into line extending the left of the Stonewall Brigade. Gibbon countered by summoning the Seventh Wisconsin, which formed opposite Lawton's men on the right of the Second Wisconsin. Jackson continued to ignore the chain of command and directly ordered Trimble's brigade to move forward and protect Lawton's left. Trimble encountered the last of Gibbon's regiments, the Sixth Wisconsin, which anchored the expanding Union battle line now stretching about one-half mile in length.

The scene that unfolded as darkness enveloped the Brawner farm inspired eloquent descriptions by those who witnessed it. "Men standing at arm's length . . . giving and taking, life for life, each resolute and determined, ceasing action only from sheer exhaustion, which was complete upon one side as upon the other," remembered one Unionist. Another Federal recalled that "the affair seemed to us like a mixture of earthquake, volcano, thunder storm and

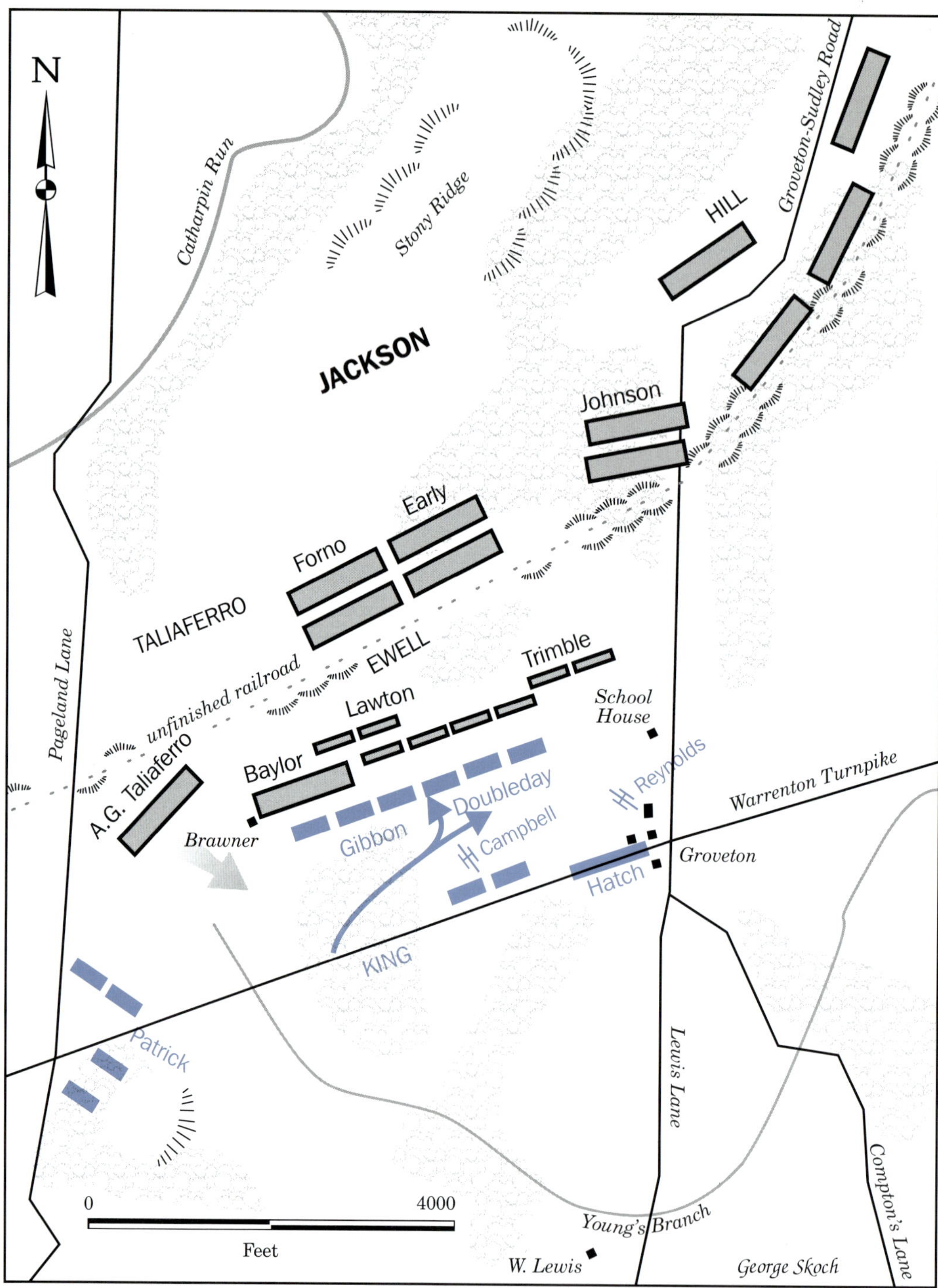

THE BATTLE OF BRAWNER FARM, AUGUST 28, 1862

After destroying Manassas Junction Jackson fell back to the old battlefield of Manassas. Reuniting his troops along Stony Ridge, north of the Warrenton Turnpike, they settled in to await the arrival of Lee and Longstreet. But before they arrived, Jackson touched off the battle on the afternoon of August 28, when the four brigades of King's Federal division moved east along the turnpike to reunite with Pope in Centreville. Jackson ordered his artillery to open fire on the enemy column. John Gibbon sent his men to capture the guns, but after advancing up the slope, they realized that they were facing several brigades of Confederate infantry. As the two sides traded volleys 75 yards apart, Abner Doubleday, whose brigade had been following Gibbon's, rushed up to help.

cyclone. Even now we can hear the . . . howls, growls, moans, screeches, screams and explosions. . . . It might have been a tune for demons to dance to." A Confederate said that "out in the sunlight, in the dying daylight, and under the stars, they stood, and although they could not advance, they would not retire. There was some discipline in this, but there was much more of true valor."

Trimble's appearance threatened to tilt the balance of power, so Gibbon turned to Doubleday for assistance. That officer (who is often incorrectly credited with inventing baseball) had anticipated Gibbon's imperilment and advanced the Fifty-sixth Pennsylvania and the Seventy-sixth New York to plug the gap between the Sixth and Seventh Wisconsins. These men arrived after dark and aimed at their invisible opponents by watching the muzzle flashes from Confederates muskets. Both Trimble and Lawton launched uncoordinated attacks against the reinforced Union battle line, receiving deadly repulses that cost one of Lawton's regiments 72 percent casualties.

Darkness and confusion prevented Stonewall from employing the additional brigades which had finally moved forward from Stony Ridge. Confederate command incapacity increased when Ewell fell with a serious wound while trying to lead an assault around the Union right flank. Three Northern bullets found Taliaferro, disabling him as well. But Taliaferro's uncle, Alexander G. Taliaferro, managed to advance three regiments of his brigade from west of the Brawner house astride the Nineteenth Indiana's axis of fire. Stuart's young cannoneer, John Pelham, assisted Taliaferro, pouring artillery projectiles into the Hoosiers from less than 100 yards uprange.

At 9:00 P.M. Gibbon and Doubleday broke off the engagement and withdrew to the turnpike in an orderly fashion, the Confederates too exhausted to pursue. The Battle of Brawner Farm had ended in a hideous tactical stalemate.

The butcher's bill told a grim tale rarely duplicated during the Civil War. Nearly one out of three battle participants fell killed or wounded at the Brawner farm, a total of 1,150 Federals and 1,250 Confederates. "In this fight there was no maneuvering and very little tactics," wrote William Taliaferro, "it was a question of endurance, and both endured." Few honors belonged to the generals directing this battle. Gibbon and Doubleday performed gallantly, but their invalided division commander played no role and neither Hatch nor Patrick lent the weight of their brigades to the equation. Jackson enjoyed a potentially decisive numerical advantage but failed to employ all his troops, because of in part the wounding of both Ewell and Taliaferro.

But if the tactical outcome at Brawner's farm left something to be desired, Jackson could not have better achieved his strategic objective. His attack on the evening of August 28 was the military equivalent of waving a red flag under John Pope's nose—and the bullish Pope reacted just as Stonewall had hoped. Rather than safely removing his army to the far side of Bull Run, the Union commander called for a concentration against Jackson at Groveton. He wrongly concluded that Gibbon's fight at the Brawner farm had arrested Jackson's retreat from Centreville and thus imagined another

Currier and Ives illustration depicting the Second Battle of Manassas. (LC)

opportunity to demolish the Valley magician. Pope issued a spate of orders on the night of the twenty-eighth aimed at surrounding Jackson and attacking him in the morning. Unfortunately, Pope predicated his strategy on several erroneous premises.

Pope assumed that McDowell and Sigel were west of Jackson blocking his retreat route toward the Bull Run Mountains, but Reynolds's division of McDowell's corps and Sigel's men were southeast of Stonewall along the Manassas-Sudley Road. The rest of McDowell's command, King and Ricketts, had already withdrawn from the turnpike before Pope's new orders could reach them, convinced by captured Confederates that Jackson had 60,000 troops ready to pounce on any nearby Federals at dawn. King headed for Manassas and Ricketts for Bristoe Station after midnight. McDowell could not bring order out of this strategic chaos because he spent the night of August 28–29 wandering lost around Prince William County in search of Pope and out of touch with his own division commanders. Worst of all, Pope's presumption that Jackson was attempting to retreat could not have been further from the truth. Stonewall was in fact anxiously anticipating the new day when Longstreet would appear and the Confederates would at last be reunited for battle. Incredibly, Pope ignored the imminent arrival of this half of his opponent's army.

Wartime sketch of the Battle of Brawner Farm by Edwin Forbes. (LC)

Those soldiers, Longstreet's 25,000 men, began their march from Thoroughfare Gap at 6:00 A.M. August 29. John Bell Hood, a sad-eyed Kentuckian who had earned a brilliant combat reputation at the head of Lee's only Texas troops, led the procession. Jackson dispatched Stuart a couple of hours later to contact Hood and direct him and the rest of Longstreet's wing into positions Stonewall had carefully preselected.

In the meantime, Jackson shuffled his depleted divisions so that they might withstand an attack should Pope become aggressive before Old Pete could arrive. Jackson noticed a large number of Federals (Sigel's corps) along the Manassas-Sudley Road in a position to threaten his left flank, so he ordered Hill's brigades to file in behind the unfinished railroad near Sudley Church with their left anchored on a rocky knoll. From here Hill could guard the emergency escape route to Aldie Gap and protect against a Federal turning movement. The thick green forest lapped against the abandoned right-of-way in this vicinity, leaving the Southern defenders particularly vulnerable to a surprise assault. Hill compensated for this unavoidable weakness by arraying his brigades in two lines, Maxcy Gregg's South Carolinians and Edward L. Thomas's Georgians at the posts of honor in the front.

Ewell's wound at the Brawner farm required that his left leg be amputated. Jackson's protégé would not return to active command until the following spring, so Stonewall named Alexander Lawton to lead Ewell's division. Lawton graduated from West Point in 1839 but resigned his

ILLUSTRATION BY EDWIN FORBES OF THE RETREATING UNION ARMY.

(LC)

commission to attend Harvard Law School. The adopted Georgian pursued a successful legal, business, and political career before his state's secession induced him to rejoin the military. Jackson placed two of Lawton's brigades in the center of his line and ordered the other two, Jubal A. Early's and Henry Forno's, to move to the far right and act as liaisons for Longstreet's units.

William E. Starke replaced the disabled Taliaferro in command of Jackson's old division. Starke had been a cotton broker in New Orleans at the outbreak of the war and had risen through the ranks to command a Louisiana brigade. His eighteen regiments held Jackson's right where expansive fields of fire and the ready-made shelter of the railroad embankment made his position relatively strong. The most vulnerable point along Starke's battle line lay on the extreme left, where his division and Lawton's intersected. Here a 75-yard low point known as "The Dump" offered little protection against attacking troops. Jackson coldly ordered the skulkers and stragglers from several commands to occupy this position as a practical object lesson in the virtue of discipline. Stuart's cavalry patrolled both of Jackson's flanks, and Stonewall unlimbered as much of his artillery as could obtain a field of fire. The Confederate line stretched some 3,000 yards defended by about 20,000 graycoats.

Pope had every intention of testing Jackson's preparedness. Disappointed to learn that King and Ricketts had abandoned the Confederate front, Pope sent word to Fitz John Porter at Manassas to attack King (Ricketts was temporarily out of the picture at Bristoe) and move north toward Gainesville to regain a blocking position beyond Jackson's right. Porter received these orders after daylight while lying on his headquarters cot elegantly draped by an imitation leopard-skin blanket. By

PUSHING ASIDE A TOKEN FEDERAL FORCE THE NIGHT BEFORE AT THOROUGHFARE GAP, LONGSTREET'S MEN MARCHED TO THE ASSISTANCE OF JACKSON, ALREADY ENGAGED AGAINST POPE'S FORCES.

(BL)

SIGEL'S ATTACK
LATE MORNING
AUGUST 29, 1862

After the fight at Brawner farm, Jackson aligned his troops behind the unfinished railroad on a front 3,000 yards long. On the morning of August 29, Federal forces began massing along Jackson's front. With orders to attack the enemy vigorously at daylight, Franz Sigel's corps advanced against the Confederate line only to be repulsed with heavy losses.

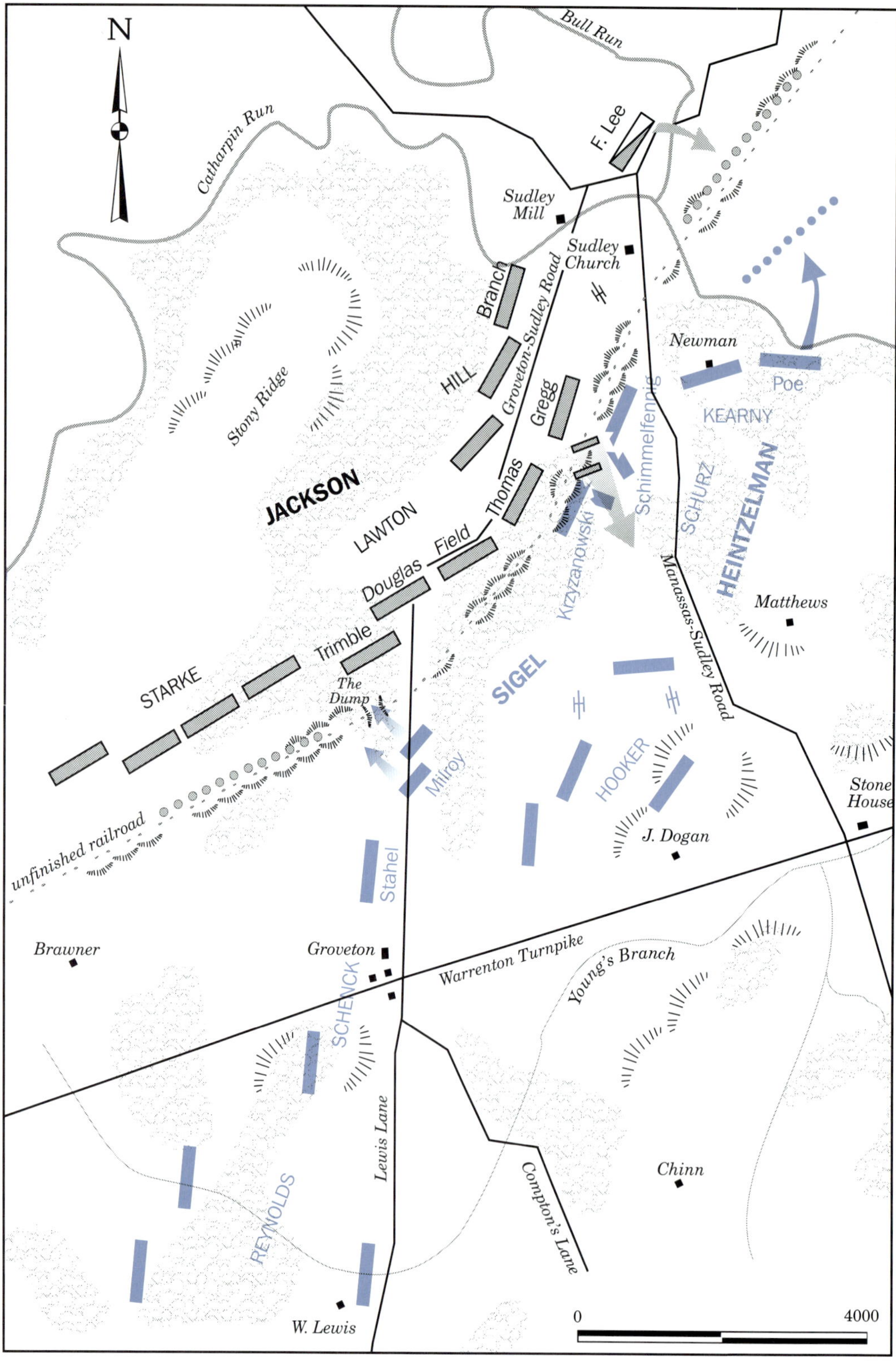

10:00 A.M. Porter, supported by King's division now under the command of John Hatch, left Manassas on the road for Gainesville to perform what Pope anticipated would be the critical movement in the ruination of Stonewall Jackson.

In the meantime, Sigel and Reynolds responded to Pope's directives to attack Jackson at daybreak. These Federals, less than 12,000 strong, had only the vaguest notion of how Jackson had deployed. Sigel therefore opted to approach the

Confederates along a broad front. Robert C. "Fighting Bob" Schenck's division supported by Reynolds would move west on the turnpike and form Sigel's left. Robert H. Milroy's Independent Brigade assumed responsibility for the center, and Carl Schurz's division advanced north on the Manassas-Sudley Road on Sigel's right. Schurz's men found Jackson first about 7:00 A.M.

A Union officer described Schurz as "a pale, wide-foreheaded, red-mustached, spectacled, effeminate-looking German. He had sharp, hazel eyes, was thin and tall, the very pattern of a visionary, itching philanthropist and philospher such as disturb society everywhere with their restless conceits and babblings." This unflattering portrait failed to do justice to one of America's leading orators and abolitionists. Like Sigel, Schurz owed his high military stature to his ethnicity and political influence, but unlike his superior, Schurz possessed some martial ability.

Schurz's two brigades skirmished heavily with Gregg and Thomas, each side committing its regiments piecemeal in the matted woods south of the unfinished railroad. "The rattling fire of skirmishers changes into crashes of musketry, regular volleys, rapidly following each other," remembered Schurz. Hill's troops blunted the Federal advance, although the Confederates were unable to exploit their advantage in the trackless terrain.

Milroy heard the sharp report of combat to his right and blindly ordered two of his regiments to move to Schurz's assistance. These troops ran into Lawton's division along the Groveton-Sudley Road and received a costly repulse, although a part of the Eighty-second Ohio briefly breached the Confederate line near The Dump. Farther to the southwest, Schenck and Reynolds fell under an intense artillery barrage and deployed in the woods around Groveton replying with counterbattery fire but choosing not to commit their infantry.

Sigel's offensive lasted until 10:00 A.M. without altering the strategic equation. Phil Kearny's division promised to terminate this impasse when it moved up opposite the left end of Hill's combat-weary line. In anticipation of receiving support from Kearny, Schurz once again lunged toward Hill's waiting brigades. The usually reliable New Jerseyian, however, failed to advance, possibly indulging a bitter grudge he nurtured against Sigel. Kearny's inaction squandered the temporary toehold won by Schurz along the unfinished railroad, and once again a Confederate counterattack drove the Yankees back through the woods. "The men still in the ranks . . . well-nigh reached the point of utter exhaustion," confessed Schurz, and by midday his battle had ended.

Sigel's efforts that morning had not been entirely in vain. He had located Jackson and "brought [him] to a stand," thought Pope, while Porter and Hatch marched toward what the Union commander considered the key point on the map. In addition to Kearny, Hooker's division and Isaac I. Stevens's brigades of Reno's corps arrived to reinforce Sigel. At 1:00 P.M. Pope appeared on the battlefield expecting that the afternoon would witness his long-deferred victory.

But as usual, John Pope forgot about Longstreet. Old Pete, in the company of General Lee, met with Jackson in midmorning near the Brawner farm while Hill's brigades engaged their Federal opponents to the east. Stonewall outlined the

Porter, supported by King's division now under the command of John Hatch, left Manassas on the road for Gainesville to perform what Pope anticipated would be the critical movement in the ruination of Stonewall Jackson.

location of his wing and, with apparent approval, the positions he recommended for Longstreet's divisions. Shortly thereafter Hood's veterans swung into view and deployed astride the turnpike facing east, loosely linking with Jackson's right flank.

James L. Kemper, a Virginia political general, filed in on Hood's right south of the turnpike. David R. "Neighbor" Jones, a thirty-seven-year-old South Carolinian, placed his division on Longstreet's right, unknowingly blocking Porter's approaching column. Cadmus Marcellus Wilcox arrived last and served as Longstreet's reserve along Pageland Lane south of the turnpike. Nineteen guns dropped trail on a ridge northeast of the Brawner farm, strengthening Longstreet's connection with Jackson. By noon the Confederates completed their arrangements. The gray line extended three miles facing east and southeast—a huge pincers aimed at Pope's left flank. Lee, Jackson, and Longstreet had completed an improbable maneuver begun more than four days earlier. Now they sought to exploit the opportunity earned by their risk-filled march.

Postwar view of the battlefield near Groveton.

(LC)

Well before Longstreet had emplaced his divisions, a handful of Stuart's cavalry blundered into Porter, Hatch, and McDowell, who were, in accordance with their morning orders, moving north on the Gainesville-Manassas Road. The scattered shots exchanged between a Pennsylvania regiment and the Confederate horsemen succeeded in halting the Union column. Porter now turned to receive a mounted courier bearing a message from Pope that would prove to be one of the most controversial documents of the campaign.

This communique became known as the "Joint Order," and Pope had written it from Centreville about 10:00 A.M. Directed to both McDowell and Porter, it reassigned Hatch's division to McDowell and attempted to clarify the goal of the movement toward Gainesville. But Pope employed such cautious and qualifying language in his directive that the Joint Order resulted in precisely the opposite of what he later professed to intend.

Apparently, Pope envisioned the scattered elements of his army converging simultaneously to challenge Jackson in his front and isolate him from Thoroughfare Gap. Sigel, Heintzelman, Reno, and Reynolds would maneuver west along the turnpike and develop Jackson's location, an operation that had already resulted in Sigel's morning combat. McDowell and Porter would reach the turnpike near Gainesville, connect with the rest of the army to the east, and strike Jackson on his supposedly vulnerable right flank.

Unfortunately for the Federals, the Joint Order as written did not convey this conception. Instead it instructed McDowell

JAMES LONGSTREET

(USAMHI)

and Porter to move toward (not to) Gainesville and "as soon as communication is established [with the other divisions] the whole command shall halt. It may be necessary to fall back behind Bull Run to Centreville tonight." After reiterating the possible need to retreat, Pope concluded by telling his two subordinates that "if any considerable advantages are to be gained from departing from this order it will not be strictly carried out." Nowhere did the Joint Order explicitly direct Porter and McDowell to attack.

While the two Federal generals digested the import and meaning of Pope's instructions, they noticed clouds of dust along the horizon on Porter's front. Jeb Stuart had decided to delay the oncoming Union column with clever theatrics until Longstreet could complete his deployment. He told one of his officers to collect a supply of branches and assign a regiment to drag the limbs across the road, creating the appearance of an approaching multitude. This stratagem worked perfectly, especially when McDowell received a report from his cavalry commander, John Buford, who had counted "seventeen regiments of infantry, one battery, and five hundred cavalry" moving through Gainesville at 8:15 that morning. Buford, of course, had discovered Longstreet's wing moving from Thoroughfare Gap, and, combined with Stuart's dusty disturbance, Buford's warning convinced Porter and McDowell that trouble loomed ahead. Mindful of Pope's requirement that they be prepared to retreat that night and the Joint Order's clause permitting discretion, McDowell and Porter made decisions completely at odds with Pope's actual, if unarticulated, thinking.

McDowell told Porter that "you are

POSTWAR VIEW OF THE GROUND LONGSTREET'S MEN OCCUPIED ON AUGUST 29.

(LC)

too far out already; this is no place to fight a battle." Exercising his regained independence from the Fifth Corps commander, McDowell ordered Hatch and Ricketts, on the march from Bristoe, to shift to the northeast, gain the Manassas-Sudley Road, and then move north to the turnpike. From there McDowell would turn westward toward the army's left and reestablish communication with Porter. Porter simply shook out a strong line of skirmishers, readied his artillery, and rested his men, awaiting clarification of the situation from Pope, McDowell, or others, while maintaining a watchful eye for Confederate activity in his front.

Porter and McDowell knew full well that Longstreet had arrived opposite Porter's line of march and that Pope's Joint Order, confidently advising that Longstreet was still thirty-six to forty-eight hours away, was painfully in error. But for some inexplicable reason McDowell failed to forward Buford's report to Pope, so the Union commander remained aggressively unaware of Porter's dilemma. Moreover, Pope believed that the Joint Order would initiate a decisive offensive by Porter and McDowell. Thus he would base his afternoon strategy around these two egregious misconceptions.

Meanwhile, Lee and Longstreet struggled with dispersing their own fog of war. Once Longstreet's divisions reached their assigned positions, Lee immediately sought to assume the offensive against the Federal left. Longstreet, however, demurred and suggested an investigation of the Union deployment both along the turnpike and south of Gainesville. Lee agreed, and in an hour Old Pete returned with worrisome news. The Federal line (Reynolds and Schenck) extended south of the turnpike covering about half of Longstreet's front. These Yankees would offer substantial if not insurmountable resistance to a Confederate attack. The bluecoats on the Gainesville-Manassas Road (Porter) must also be neutralized, thought Longstreet, or he would risk their intervention on his right flank and rear during any attack eastward on the turnpike. The time, Longstreet insisted, was not right for his wing to move forward.

Lee strenuously dissented and offered other expedients to Longstreet, who steadfastly clung to his conclusion. Marse Robert authorized his engineers to reexamine the ground, but before they could depart Stuart reported that the Union force on the Gainesville-Manassas Road did indeed pre-

The Sudley-Manassas Road looking north toward the Warrenton Turnpike. (LC)

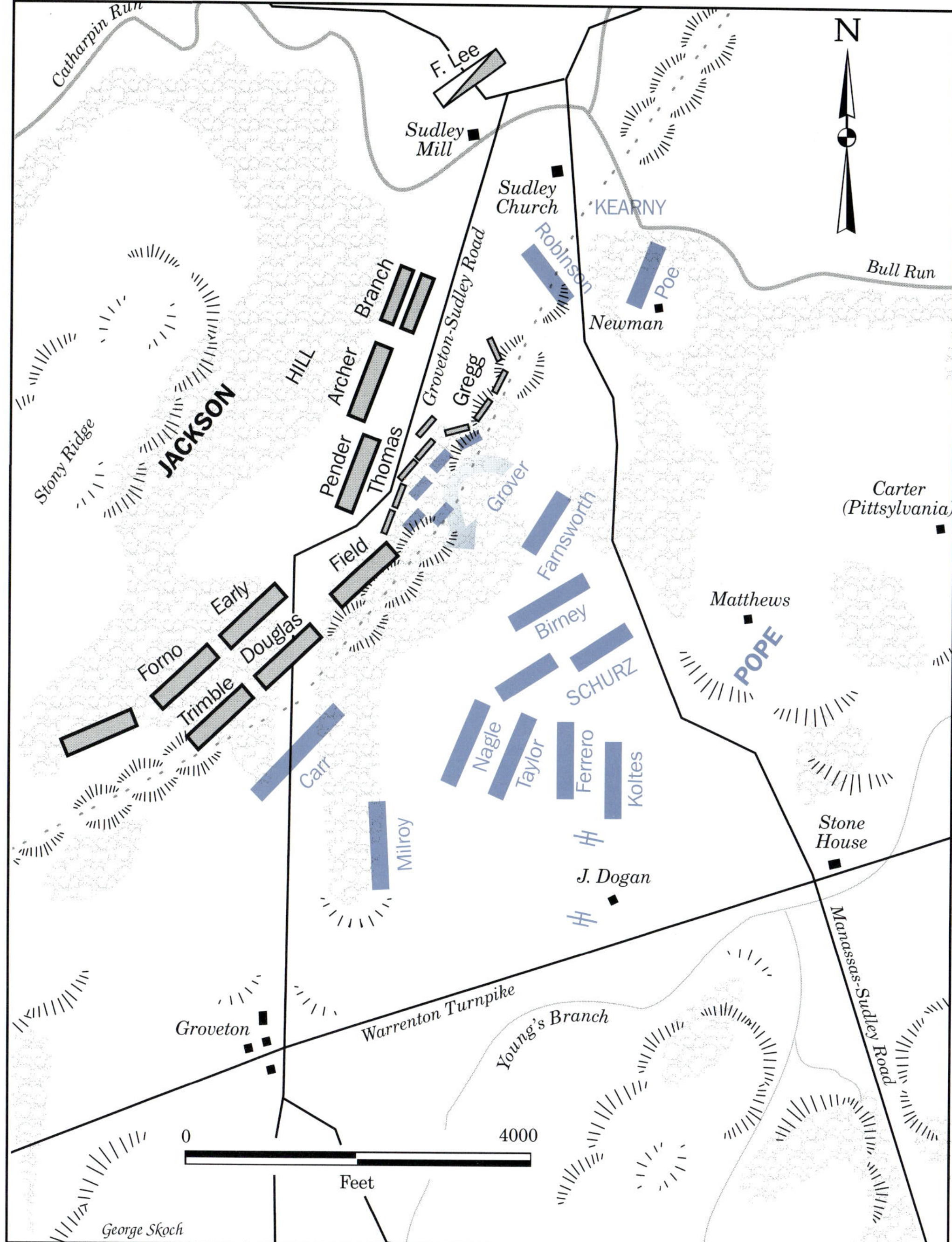

GROVER'S ATTACK, 3:00 P.M. AUGUST 29, 1862

With 1,500 men Cuvier Grover advanced against the Confederate line. Quickly Grover's men stormed over the top of the railroad embankment and proceeded to shatter the Confederate position. With no support, Grover's attack faltered. The brigade soon fell back to where it had started, leaving behind 487 men killed, wounded, and missing.

sent a formidable threat. This ended the Lee-Longstreet debate for the moment. There would be no attack until Lee could learn more about those Federals. Thus Porter's mere presence undercut Longstreet's offensive capabilities on the afternoon of August 29, but John Pope expected more of the Fifth Corps than that—much more.

Pope, of course, predicated the rest of his day's battle plans on his anticipation of Porter's pivotal assault against Stonewall Jackson's "exposed" right flank, a delusion of the first magnitude. Pope would authorize four separate offensives against Jackson's front for the sole purpose of occupying Stonewall's attention until Porter delivered his fatal blow. Despite the hollow premise of this strategy, Pope's afternoon offensives on August 29 severely tested Jackson's hard-pressed divisions.

Shortly after midday, Pope instructed Stevens and Hooker to relieve the exhausted Schurz on the Union right. These officers obeyed, but Schurz's withdrawal permitted Edward Thomas to plant the Confederate banner along the railroad cut in his front. Thomas, however, allowed a 125-yard gap to open between his regiments and Gregg's, a significant oversight that would soon threaten the viability of the Confederate line.

With bayonets fixed along a battlefront one-quarter mile wide, Grover's determined warriors charged with a yell, rapidly reaching Thomas's startled defenders.

Cuvier Grover's brigade of Hooker's division struck that gap about 3:00 P.M. in the first of Pope's afternoon attacks. This young New Englander commanded five regiments, only 1,500 men, but expected to receive support from Kearny's division. Wishing to avoid the open ground in his immediate front and to form a connection with Kearny's brigades, Grover angled his unit toward the right. Although Kearny failed to advance once again, Grover's course brought him, purely by accident, to the gap between Thomas and Gregg.

With bayonets fixed along a battlefront one-quarter mile wide, Grover's determined warriors charged with a yell, rapidly reaching Thomas's startled defenders. "I was within two rods of the enemy's line before I was aware of it," admitted a Massachusetts volunteer. A soldier in the Forty-fifth Georgia recalled that "I turned and saw the whole regiment getting away, and I followed the example in tripple [*sic*] quick time." In a matter of moments, Grover had overrun Thomas and isolated Gregg. This was the time when fresh Union troops might have effected the permanent dislocation of Jackson's left flank.

But Pope never intended to devote his major effort to this end of the battlefield. Grover's success represented a mere diversion, although Kearny's nonparticipation contributed to the certainty that Grover's gains would be temporary. Gregg responded to the crisis on his right by committing three regiments to assail Grover's exposed flank. North Carolinians under Dorsey Pender appeared from Hill's reserve line to press Grover in front. "The effect was terrible," shuddered a soldier from the First Massachusetts. "Men dropped in scores, writhing and trying to crawl back, or lying immovable and stone-dead where they fell." Within 30 minutes of their advance, Grover's men returned to their jump-off points, leaving behind one-third of their comrades killed, wounded, or captured.

Pope ordered John Reynolds to conduct the next spoiling attack south of the turnpike. Reynolds, who had watched Longstreet's wing deploy late in the morning, reported that a large Confederate force menaced his front but dutifully obeyed his superior's command. Predictably, Reynolds encountered Longstreet's extensive lines almost immediately. He promptly canceled his demonstration, reiterating to Pope the reality of the situation. The Union commander dismissed Reynolds's concern as a

CUVIER GROVER

(USAMHI)

case of mistaken identity, absurdly insisting that the Pennsylvanian had actually seen Porter's divisions preparing for their imminent attack against Jackson's flank.

In the meantime, Jesse Reno complied with Pope's order to occupy the Rebels in his sector by advancing a brigade under James Nagle. Nagle's experience mirrored that of Grover an hour earlier. His three large regiments pierced the Confederate center near the Groveton-Sudley Road and swept Trimble's brigade from the railroad embankment. But without supports, Nagle fell victim to a Confederate counterattack led by a Marylander named Bradley Johnson. Johnson landed on Nagle's left flank and, assisted by a fresh brigade of Louisianians, drove Nagle back from whence he came. The Confederates pursued into the open fields where Union artillery halted their advance. During this charge a Virginian in Johnson's brigade remembered hearing "a thud on my right, as if one had been struck with a heavy fist. Looking around, I saw a man at my side who was standing erect, with his head off and a stream of blood spurting a foot or more from his neck." Three other Confederates had been killed by this same cannon ball.

Pope now consolidated his lines, placed McDowell's newly arrived divisions of Hatch and Ricketts on Henry Hill in support of the justifiably nervous Reynolds, and sent positive orders to Porter to begin his attack. "Your line of march brings you on the enemy's right flank. I desire you to push forward into action at once on the enemy's flank, and, if possible, on his rear, keeping your right in communication with General Reynolds." Pope wrote this directive at 4:30 P.M. but his aide, Pope's nephew, lost his way and did not deliver the message until two hours later. Of course, Pope's instructions were no less impractical in the evening than they were in the afternoon and Porter could not execute them.

It would be several more hours, however, before the sanguine Union commander would realize this. Expecting Porter's long-anticipated offensive at last to be imminent, Pope renewed his order to Kearny to assail Jackson's far left, providing what Pope thought would be simultaneous pressure against both Confederate flanks. Kearny assembled ten regiments, some 2,700 men from three of his brigades, and prepared to move both astride the unfinished railroad and against

1880s VIEW OF HENRY HILL, SITE OF THE CLOSING ACTION DURING THE BATTLE.

(LC)

KEARNY'S ATTACK, 5:00 P.M. AUGUST 29, 1862
Having been hard-pressed all day, the men of A. P. Hill's division had to endure one final Union onslaught. This time Phil Kearny surged against the Confederate line with nearly 3,000 men. Kearny's men hit the unfinished railroad and swept everything before them. The Confederates regrouped and pushed the Federals back in a vicious hand-to-hand fight that marked the final Union attack on Jackson's front that day.

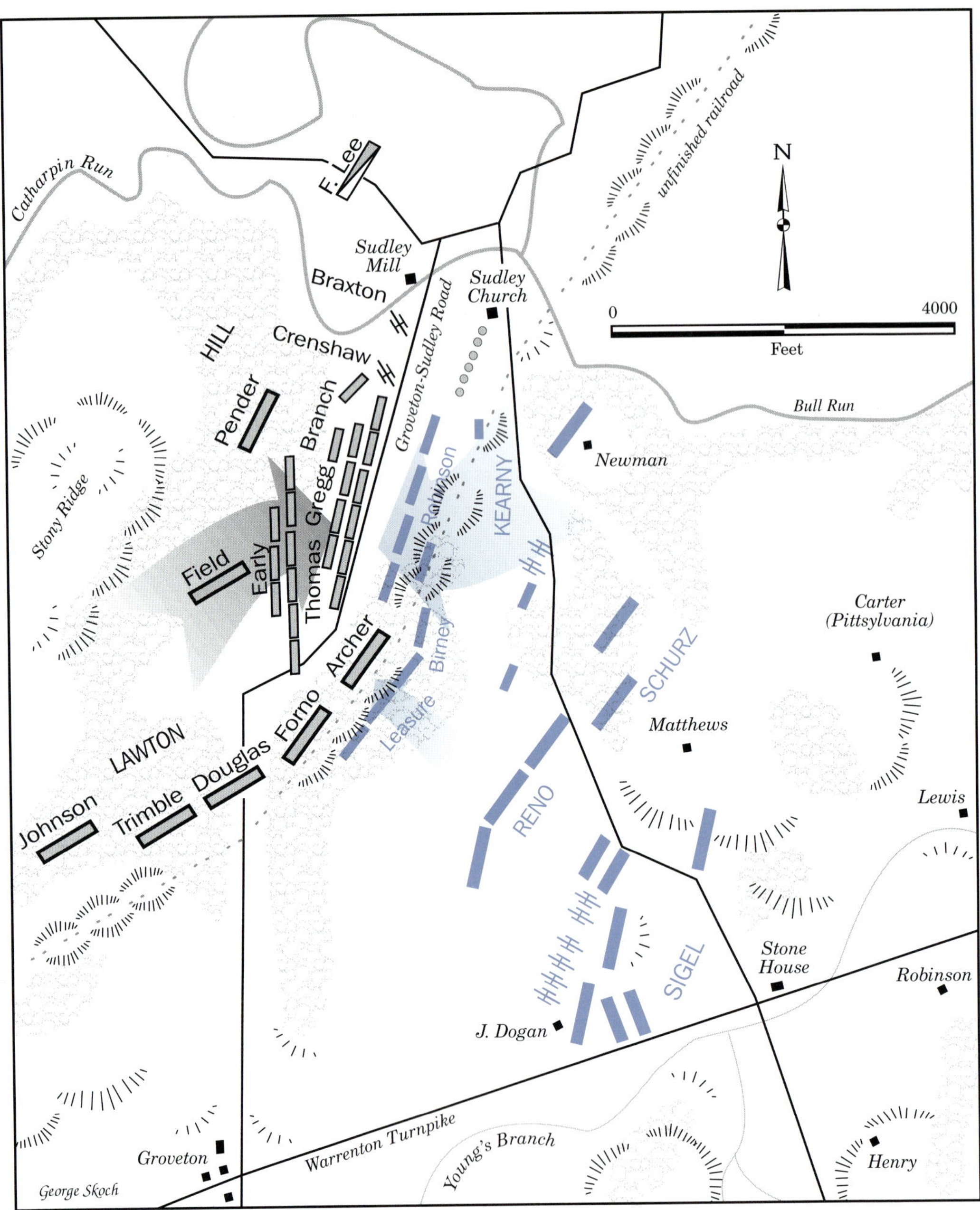

Jackson's front, employing support from twenty pieces of artillery.

Phil Kearny arrived at Manassas with a reputation as solid as any officer's in the Union army. "He . . . was the finest specimen of the fighting soldier I had ever seen," gushed an admirer, while Pope praised him as one who "never seemed so much at home and so cheerful and confident as in battle." Thus far on August 29, however, Kearny had done nothing but disappoint those who depended on him. The assault that began at 5:00 P.M. did something to redeem Kearny's earlier failures.

The Confederates who would meet Kearny's assault, the men of Hill's Light Division, had suffered more that day than any of Jackson's commands. Four of Hill's six brigades had sustained significant casualties or disorganization as a result of repulsing Sigel's, Grover's, and Nagle's offensives. Maxcy Gregg's Palmetto Staters, anchoring Hill's (and Jackson's) far left, had nearly exhausted their ammunition and had absorbed heavy losses. Hill sent a courier to Jackson to report his division's predicament, to which Jackson replied, "Tell him if they attack him again he must beat them." Stonewall decided to ride back with the messenger and speak directly to Hill. Jackson met his subordinate partway down the line and told the red-shirted Virginian that "if you are attacked again you will beat the enemy back." Just then the crash of musketry announced the inauguration of Kearny's assault. "Here it comes," shouted Hill. "I'll expect you to beat them," thundered Jackson in reply.

Kearny had orchestrated an effective envelopment which encountered Gregg's weary regiments and a reserve brigade under James J. Archer. Kearny told a regimental officer to adjust his unit in a particular alignment, then "charge, and the day is ours. I will support you handsomely." Gregg's brigade absorbed additional losses as their fire-eating commander waved his oversized sword and advised the survivors to "let us die here, my men, let us die here."

Kearny called on Daniel Leasure's brigade of Reno's corps to move in on his left. "That is your line of advance," Kearny barked. "Sweep everything before you." Leasure's Pennsylvanians and New Yorkers pushed ahead to the unfinished railroad, and Hill's line faced imminent dissolution. But typical of Confederate leadership that day, reinforcements appeared at the right place and in the nick of time. The last of Hill's untested brigades, North Carolinians under Lawrence O'B. Branch, piled into Kearny and Leasure halting the Federal advance but unable to expel the attacking bluecoats. That job belonged to Jubal Early, who had moved from Jackson's far right in the morning to a reserve position in Lawton's line in mid-afternoon and now to the critical point of danger. According to a soldier in Gregg's brigade, Early's troops "came rushing up, comparatively fresh for the work, and cheering us as they advanced . . . with a wild Confederate yell, rushed upon [the Northerners]. The Federals halted, turned, and fled."

On the Union side, one enervated Yankee remembered that "our guns had become so fouled with burnt powder that we had to jam the rammer against a tree to drive the ball home." A Confederate recalled that "all the sounds of Babel roared about us. There was a perfect death storm all around." This vicious fighting, the most serious of the entire day, ended like the rest of Pope's August 29 offensives—in ultimate Union repulse. Gregg's brigade had completely emptied its cartridge boxes and lost fully half its men while the rest of the Light Division suffered severely as well, but Kearny's threat had ended. When Hill sent word to Jackson that the enemy had retired, Stonewall allowed a rare smile to brighten his countenance. "Tell him I knew he would do it."

Meanwhile, on the Confederate right, Lee and Longstreet continued to fret about Porter's looming presence and shifted Longstreet's troops to prevent the Federals from turning the Rebel right flank. But by 4:00 P.M. Old Pete had spied the dust clouds raised by McDowell's divisions as they tramped away from Porter toward the Manassas-

PHIL KEARNY
(USAMHI)

Hood's line overlapped the narrow Union front and forced the Northerners to melt backward into the night.

Sudley Road. Longstreet recognized this as a signal that the Yankees had partially withdrawn from his front and so reported to Lee. Marse Robert immediately revived the attack scenario he had so reluctantly postponed a few hours before, but once again Longstreet tempered his commander's aggressiveness. The sun was too low, argued Longstreet, to undertake a major offensive. Why not conduct a reconnaissance in force and move into position to begin the assault in the morning? "After a moment's hesitation" Lee assented to this plan and Longstreet selected Hood's brigades supported by portions of Wilcox's and Kemper's divisions to make the probe. The advance south of the turnpike began about sunset.

In the meantime, Pope continued to operate in a strategic fantasy land. Reacting to Kearny's initial success and misinterpreting the incidental movement of Confederate ambulances west on the turnpike, the Union chieftain concluded that the Confederates were once again on the retreat. He assigned Hatch's division, the veterans of the previous evening's fight at the Brawner farm, to pursue along the turnpike. Hatch sent two brigades forward, and as they crested the hill overlooking Groveton they ran headlong into Hood's approaching Confederates.

A. P. HILL

(MC)

"The enemy . . . were rather more combative than we presumed retreating forces usually to be," one Federal noted wryly. Hood's line overlapped the narrow Union front and forced the Northerners to melt backward into the night. It became "so dark that one flag could not be distinguished from another, nor the Yankee troops from Southern soldiers," complained a Texan, but before the firing died away the Confederates had captured a Union artillery piece and seized the ground needed to launch an attack at dawn.

But Longstreet's subordinates, Hood, Wilcox, and brigade commander Evander M. Law, strongly recommended that no such assault take place. The Federals apparently held the area in force so a forward movement might jeopardize the security of the Confederate flanks. They persuaded the cautious Longstreet, who in turn convinced Lee to cancel the offensive for a third time. Shortly after midnight the Southerners withdrew from their advanced positions and resumed the defensive posture they had occupied during the afternoon.

McDowell had not accompanied Hatch on the ill-fated "pursuit" that night. Instead he rode to Pope's headquarters and, among other things, told the Union commander of Buford's morning observation of heavy Confederate reinforcements at Gainesville. Pope at last acknowledged that Longstreet had arrived but wrongly assumed that Old Pete would merely reinforce Jackson's battered lines until the Confederates could execute a wholesale skedaddle in the morning. Once again, John Pope had misread the strategic picture.

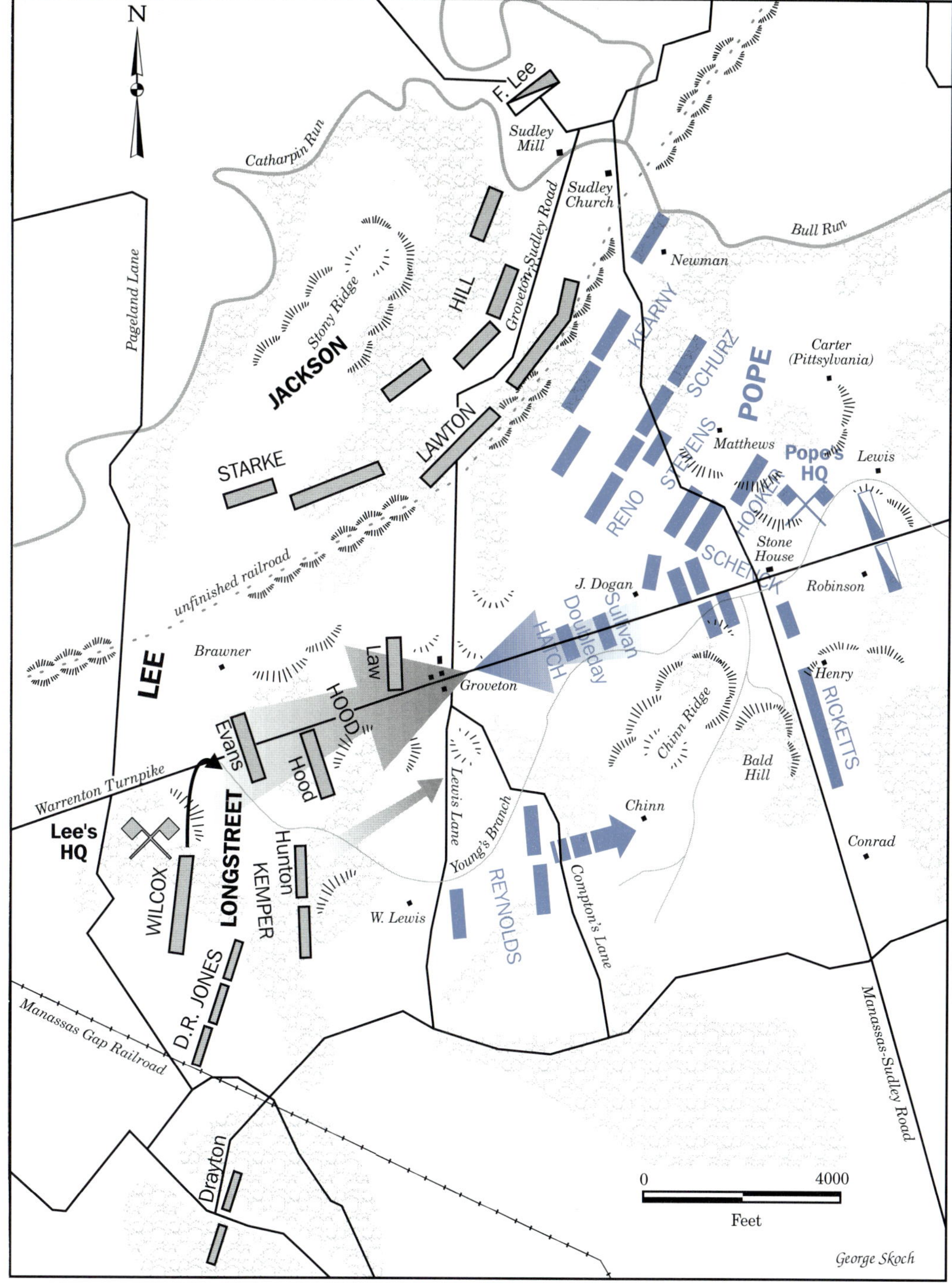

HOOD'S TWILIGHT CLASH, 7:00 P.M. AUGUST 29, 1862

Uncertain about the Union army's position, John Bell Hood's division probed eastward along the Warrenton Turnpike. Meanwhile, Pope ordered John Hatch's division westward along the turnpike in the mistaken belief that the Confederates were retreating. Approaching the Groveton crossroads, Hatch's troops clashed with Hood's force in a brief but violent encounter.

He did understand that Fitz John Porter had utterly failed to undertake the major offensive of the day. Angrily denouncing Porter as incompentent at best and traitorous at worst, at 8:50 P.M. Pope forwarded peremptory orders for Porter to join the rest of the army by morning. The Fifth Corps would participate in Pope's plans to destroy Lee on August 30 whether the Confederates opted to stay and fight or, more likely, attempted to escape. In a campaign defined by Pope's misguided generalship, this decision stands out. The prudent course on the night of August 29 dictated that Pope fall back behind Bull Run and unite with the rest of McClellan's army, the campaign's primary objective. No longer did Pope enjoy numerical superiority over Lee nor did his army's position provide him any compelling geographical

THE NOW SILENT FIELDS OF HENRY HILL. (NPS)

advantage. Moreover, Pope had every reason to believe that melding his army with McClellan's would require a retrograde movement because Little Mac had done nothing to suggest that he planned to reinforce Pope any time soon.

William Franklin's corps of the Army of the Potomac had arrived in Alexandria on August 26, and Edwin V. Sumner's appeared two days later. Together these units numbered 25,000 men, a potentially decisive force if they could join Pope at Manassas. But despite General Halleck's renewed instructions on August 28 to rush Franklin and Sumner to Pope's aid, McClellan explained that his artillery, cavalry, and transportation were all inadequate to justify an advance. On August 29 the "Young Napoleon" at last permitted Franklin to leave the Washington defenses but halted him at Annandale, barely seven miles from his starting point and nowhere near a position to influence affairs on the battlefield. Franklin's men listened passively to the distant rumble of combat while McClellan wrote an unreserved letter to his wife in which he called Pope a fool. That night Franklin corresponded with Pope under orders from McClellan offering to send supply wagons forward to the Army of Virginia if Pope would kindly provide a cavalry escort!

The temptation is great to accuse George McClellan of treacherously withholding assistance from his brother officer at a time of crisis. McClellan undeniably abhorred Pope and saw the Illinoisan as a rival who threatened to supplant him as Union commander in the east. But Little Mac's reluctance to hasten toward Bull Run stemmed more from his natural inclination for overcaution than from bad faith. He believed that Washington's security depended on keeping the remainder of his army intact and that to hurry reinforcements to Pope would entail too great a risk. When McClellan told Lincoln on August 29 that it might be wise "to leave Pope to get out of his scrape, and at once use all our means to make the capital perfectly safe," he reflected his sincere if tragically misguided vision of the proper course of action.

While McClellan agonized in a paralyzing sea of pessimism, John Pope saw

JOHN BELL HOOD (MC)

nothing but opportunity on the morning of August 30. Richard H. Anderson's Confederate division, the missing element of Longstreet's wing, had arrived at 3:00 A.M. after a seventeen-mile march and halted on the ridge east of Groveton. Recognizing their isolated position, Anderson's men fell back at dawn, a movement spotted by one of Hatch's brigadiers. Of course, the rest of Longstreet's troops had also withdrawn after dark in accordance with Lee's decision to cancel his morning offensive. When combined with credulous intelligence from paroled Union prisoners that the Rebels planned a wholesale retreat, Anderson's pullout convinced Pope that his prediction had come true.

The Union commander called an 8:00 A.M. council of war at his headquarters above the Stone House on Buck Hill to finalize the army's plans. Pope's subordinates did not share their general's rosy interpretation of the strategic situation and persuaded him to poke and jab against the unfinished railroad to test his conviction that the Rebels were on the run. By 10:00 A.M. both Ricketts and Stevens had located Jackson's men as firmly ensconced in their defensive lairs as they had been the previous day. Reynolds confirmed that the Confederates remained in great strength and threatening posture south of the turnpike. But when McDowell and Heintzelman somehow failed to discover Jackson's battle lines during a personal reconnaisance late in the morning and an escaped Union prisoner reiterated earlier tales of impending Confederate retreat, Pope equivocated no longer. The Union commander issued orders for Porter's divisions, supported by Hatch and Reynolds, to advance west along the turnpike, while Ricketts, in the company of Kearny and Hooker, would go forward on the Union right to execute what Pope envisioned as the grand pursuit of a desperate enemy.

FITZ JOHN PORTER

(USAMHI)

The temptation is great to accuse George McClellan of treacherously withholding assistance from his brother officer at a time of crisis.

The Confederates, of course, cherished no desire to escape Pope. In fact, "when Saturday [August 30] broke, we were a little apprehensive that Pope was going to get away from us," admitted James Longstreet. Jackson believed that there would be no battle that day, but at his own council of war, Lee expressed the hope that Pope would renew his attacks and create an opportunity for Longstreet to counterpunch against the Union left. Absent a Federal offensive, Lee instructed Jackson to abandon the unfinished railroad after dark and conduct another far-reaching movement around the Union right flank, interposing his wing between Pope and Washington. Longstreet would create a diversion with a late afternoon demonstration. In the meantime, Lee sent eighteen pieces of artillery under Stephen D. Lee (no relation) to the high ground northeast of the Brawner farm in perfect position to rake the open fields in front of Jackson's right. Neither Jackson nor Longstreet made any significant changes in the deployment of their troops, both officers being content to wait for Pope to begin the ball or idle away the day until the Confederate initiative could begin in the evening.

Pope had no inkling of either the Confederates' plans or dispositions, and the pursuit he ordered shortly after noon never materialized. Porter's corps, minus one brigade which lost its way during the march to the battlefield before dawn, had shifted to the woods north of the turnpike near Groveton and could not easily maneuver back to the highway to commence the chase. Ricketts did move forward but met an instant repulse from Jackson's line. Reynolds then reported to Pope that the Confederates south of the turnpike presented a greater danger than ever. Reluctantly Pope conceded that Lee had not abandoned the field but saw no reason to surrender his cherished desire to thrash the Confederates.

SKIRMISHERS FROM BERDAN'S SHARPSHOOTERS MOVED FORWARD BEFORE PORTER'S ATTACK.

(*CO. D SHARPSHOOTER* BY DON TROIANI, COURTESY OF HISTORICAL ART PRINTS LIMITED, SOUTHBURY, CONNECTICUT)

At 1:00 P.M. he sent orders to Porter to use his two divisions plus Hatch's to assault the Confederates in his front. Like his offensives of the previous day, Pope provided no support for Porter's attack, prepared no distractions elsewhere along the line, and issued no directives for what to do should the charge be successful. He did grant Reynolds permission to retire eastward to Chinn Ridge from his vulnerable position at Groveton and authorized one additional brigade under Nathaniel McLean of Schenk's division to reinforce Reynolds. This meant that the Federals posted 8,000 men south of the turnpike to oppose Longstreet's 30,000.

Porter struggled with the wooded terrain east of Groveton and required nearly two hours to arrange his 10,000 troops for the assault. Henry Weeks and Charles Roberts placed their brigades on the left and in the center of Porter's formation. Hatch's division assumed responsibility for Porter's right. Two brigades of regular United States Army troops under George Sykes filed into a reserve line poised to exploit any local advantage earned by the initial attackers. On his own initiative after Reynolds's departure, Gouverneur K. Warren shifted his tiny brigade of two New York regiments to a position south of the turnpike. Warren joined Battery D of the Fifth United States Artillery under young Charles Hazlett, who had emplaced his six guns on a prominent knoll overlooking Groveton. Only a handful of additional Union artillery could find locations from which to strengthen the infantry attack. Porter's foot soldiers would have to carry the burden virtually alone.

The Confederates targeted by Porter's assault belonged to Starke's division, which formed in parallel lines concealed by the unfinished railroad and the woods beyond. Louisiana planter Leroy A. Stafford commanded Starke's old brigade of Bayou Staters who defended the line near The Dump. To Stafford's right, Bradley Johnson's Virginians occupied a pronounced portion of the railroad bed known as the Deep Cut. Brawner farm veterans from A. G. Taliaferro's command and the Stonewall Brigade crouched in the forest on Johnson's right. A Maryland battery provided direct support to the Confederate battle line, which fronted an open field varying in depth from 300 to 600 yards, the last 150 yards of which pitched sharply uphill.

from cannon and muskets. "The shouts and yells from both sides were indescribably savage," remembered one New Yorker. "It seemed like the popular idea of pandemonium made real, and . . . it is scarcely too much to say that we were really transformed for the time, from a lot of good-natured boys to the most blood-thirsty of demoniacs."

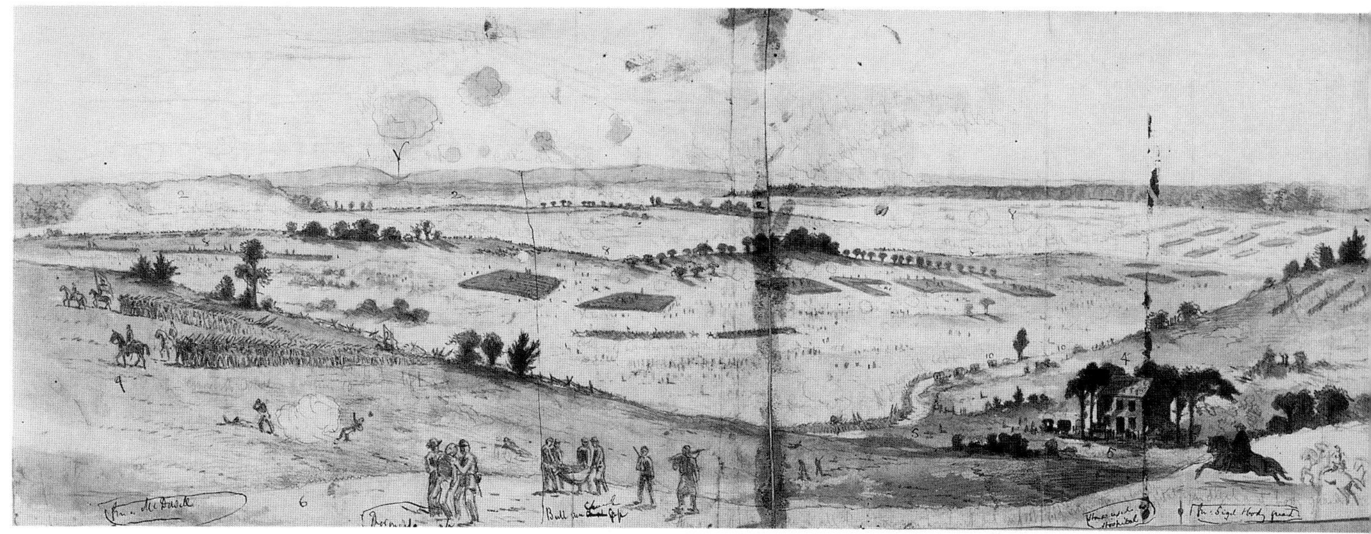

SKETCH OF PORTER'S ATTACK AS SEEN FROM HENRY HILL.

(LC)

At 2:30 P.M. members of Hiram Berdan's colorful Union sharpshooters scaled the fence along the Groveton-Sudley Road and entered the pasture owned by a widow named Lucinda Dogan, whose substantial holdings surrounded the village of Groveton. Joined by two New York regiments, the green-uniformed marksmen found slight shelter in a dry streambed (now called Schoolhouse Branch) and skirmished with Starke's Confederates for nearly thirty minutes. Then Porter's lead ranks emerged from the woods and began their long trek across the killing fields of the Dogan farm.

Hatch's men on the Union right faced the shortest exposure in the open ground. The soldiers of the Twenty-fourth and Thirtieth New York toppled the fence paralleling the road and hastened for the Confederate positions under an intense fire

The Federals managed to reach the edge of the railroad bed separated from their gray-clad opponents by the width of the embankment. Several particularly brave Union officers entered the fight on horseback, making themselves conspicuous targets and attracting grudging admiration from nearby Confederates. After a momentary debate, the Southerners decided that this Yankee gallantry did not warrant a reprieve from the hazards of war, and Rebel rifles tumbled the courageous New Yorkers from their saddles. The surviving Federals clutched the ground below the embankment and formed a rough line within whispering distance of the Louisianians.

To Hatch's left, Roberts and Weeks appeared on the naked tract opposite Bradley Johnson's waiting Virginians. "The advance began in magnificent style, lines

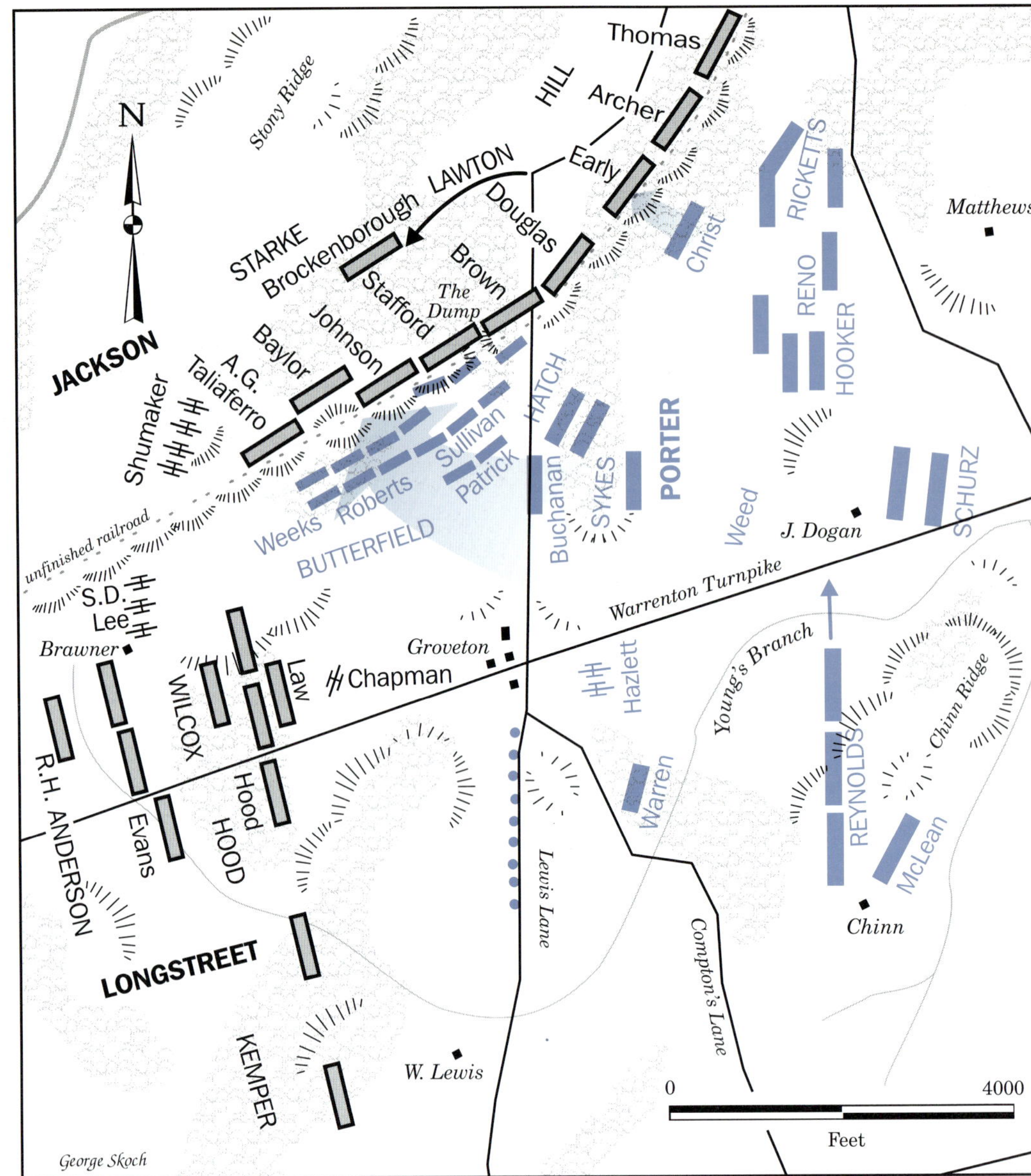

PORTER'S ATTACK, 3:00 P.M. AUGUST 30, 1862

Like an avalanche the men of Porter's corps descended into the fields of the Dogan farm. Hatch's brigade on the Union right faced the shortest stretch of exposed ground and quickly reached the railroad embankment, only to be pinned down. Butterfield's division on the Union left had the farthest distance to cover in order to reach the Confederate line. The Union ranks on the left were constantly raked by S. D. Lee's guns on the heights north of the Brawner farm. With their ammunition running low, some Confederates along the unfinished railroad were reduced to fighting with rocks. As Southern reinforcements arrived on the front, Porter's men fell back from the railroad, their attack in shambles.

as straight as an arrow, all fringed with glittering bayonets and fluttering with flags," wrote a Confederate observer. "But the march had scarce begun when little puffs of smoke appeared, dotting the field in rapid succession just over the heads of the men, and as the lines moved on, where each little puff had been, lay a pile of bodies, and half a dozen or more staggering figures standing around leaning on their muskets and then slowly limping back to the rear." These Unionists had to traverse nearly a quarter-mile of shelterless terrain before gaining the unfinished railroad, and they paid dearly for the achievement. As they reached Johnson's position, the Confederates leveled their rifles and unleashed a withering volley. "The first line of the attacking column looked as if it had been struck by a blast from a tempest, and had been blown away," marveled one Southerner.

But the Federal momentum penetrated Johnson's line, routing the Forty-eighth Virginia and compromising the rest of the unit. In rushed the Stonewall Brigade led by its intrepid commander, William S. H. Baylor. The Valley veterans restored the Confederate battlefront at heavy cost, including Colonel Baylor, who died with the flag of the Thirty-third Virginia wrapped around his body. As was the case on Hatch's sector, the Federals near the Deep Cut retained their advanced positions exchanging a ceaseless fire with their well-sheltered opponents behind the railroad excavation just a few yards away.

Jackson clearly needed help. Stonewall's three divisions had marched more than fifty miles in thirty-four hours, destroyed the Union supply base, fought delaying actions at Bristoe and Manassas, engaged Pope's army at the Brawner farm, and fought along Stony Ridge for two days. His bloodied and battered brigades had thus far carried the campaign virtually alone, and the time had come for Longstreet to contribute. Jackson dispatched the future memoirist Henry Kyd Douglas to ask Old Pete for assistance.

Longstreet also recognized that the moment had arrived for his divisions to uncoil. But he reasoned that sending infantry to Jackson would consume too much time. Instead he ordered additional batteries to drop trail in support of S. D. Lee's guns at the Brawner farm. These artillerists enjoyed an unobstructed view of the pastureland across which any Union reinforcements must move to reach their comrades huddled along the embankment. This same fire would inflict appalling casualties on any Northerners who attempted to retreat from their toeholds to the safety of the Groveton Woods. Within twenty minutes of the commencement of Porter's attack, the ground between the Groveton-Sudley Road and the unfinished railroad exploded from the effect of Lee's cannonade.

When fresh Union troops attempted to run this gauntlet, iron missles from Confederate guns cut them to pieces. "Longstreet's batteries . . . were enfilading the approaching troops with solid shot, shell, and sections . . . of railroad iron, which tore up the earth frightfully, and was death to any living thing that they might touch on their passage." Porter opted not to commit Sykes to the relief of Roberts and Weeks, but he did allow additional units from Hatch's division to attempt to rescue the two regiments clinging to the unfinished railroad on the Union right. As these Federals raced across the fields absorbing a brutal enfilading artillery fire, they encountered the cataclysmic presence of fresh Confederate infantry released by Lawton's division to support Stafford's hard-pressed left flank. "They were so thick it was just impossible to miss them," said one Southerner. "What a slaughter of men that was."

By this time, Porter had surrendered the initiative. He chose not to reinforce

Robert E. Lee and his staff on the battlefield at Manassas. (LC)

S. D. Lee's well-placed artillery decimated the ranks of Porter's corps. (LC)

Union troops of Porter's corps fell like tenpins before an expert player.

(LC)

failure any longer and essentially abandoned to their fates the four Union brigades who had clawed their way to the front. Had he known, however, how severely his assaults had stressed Jackson's line, he might have continued the offensive. Stafford's and Johnson's brigades had completely expended their ammunition and relied on hurling large rocks across the embankment to defend their position. The rest of Stonewall's wing had nearly reached its capacity to sustain combat. But the appearance of Charles Field's Virginia brigade of A. P. Hill's division ultimately tipped the balance in favor of the Confederates. "At last physical strength and moral endurance alike gave way before the terrible effect of our fire," boasted a Rebel officer, "and the whole [Union] force fled in disorderly rout to the rear."

Soldiers of Porter's corps charged forward against Jackson's line. The Confederates, protected by the unfinished railroad, shattered this attack in less than thirty minutes.

(LC)

Porter's advanced brigades lost heavily during their retreat from the unfinished railroad. Some of Starke's men, caught up in the passion of victory, began a spontaneous pursuit that met a decided repulse from Union reserves posted along the Groveton-Sudley Road. The Confederates returned to their original positions and witnessed an unspeakable scene of horror. "The Yankees in front of the RR . . . were lying in heaps," recalled a Louisianian. "Some with their brains oozing out; some with the face shot off; others with their bowels protruding; others with shattered limbs."

The survivors of Porter's attack found welcome refuge in the Groveton Woods east of the Groveton-Sudley Road. Sigel's corps, Milroy's brigade, and Federal cavalry units supported Sykes and the reserve regiments of Hatch's division to stem the tide of refugees. Jackson's exhaustion rendered him unable to organize a rapid pursuit, allowing Porter to stabilize the tactical situation north of the turnpike. But to Irvin McDowell the situation appeared grim. Fearing for the safety of Porter's corps, McDowell ordered Reynolds to cross the turnpike from Chinn Ridge. Not only was such a precaution totally unnecessary but Reynolds's departure left only 2,200 men south of the highway, McLean's and Warren's brigades, to oppose more than ten times that many Confederates. McDowell's decision would be the most serious tactical error of the day because those Confederates were about to erupt onto the tactical stage at Second Manassas with dramatic effect.

Lee and Longstreet both concluded that the moment had indisputably arrived to commence the massive Confederate offensive that Lee had hoped to begin the previous day. Its goal, ironically, would be Henry Hill, the key terrain at the First Battle of Manassas. Confederate control of this lofty plateau would confine the Federals to the north side of the turnpike and deny them their retreat routes across Bull Run. The lure of complete victory thus animated Longstreet's five divisions, whose enemy would be the descending sun as well as the Northern army.

Longstreet's wing extended nearly a mile and a half from the Brawner farm on its left to the Manassas Gap Railroad on its right. The distance to Henry Hill varied from one and a half to two miles and the intervening landscape contained numerous small streams, some heavy woods, and intermediate ridges. Old Pete recognized that his troops would find it impossible to maintain an unbroken attack formation so success would depend on speed, good judgment, and hard fighting by his individual subordinate commanders. John Bell Hood's division, led by the Texas Brigade and supported by Nathan G. "Shanks" Evans's South Carolinians, would begin the assault from the left of Longstreet's line, nearest the turnpike. Kemper's division would move on Hood's right with D. R. Jones's brigades in support of Kemper's right. The rest of Longstreet's wing would provide a ready reserve. "The heavy fumes of gunpowder hanging about our ranks, as stimulating as sparkling wine, charged the atmosphere with the light and splendor of battle," recalled Longstreet, and "as the orders were given . . . twenty-five thousand braves moved in line as by a single impulse."

At 4:00 P.M. Hood's five regiments (only three of them Texans) stepped out "with all the steadiness and firmness that characterizes war-worn veterans." Their first opposition would come from the Tenth and Fifth New York regiments, Warren's 1,000 men deployed in skirmish

WITH THEIR AMMUNITION EXHAUSTED, CONFEDERATES ALONG THE UNFINISHED RAILROAD HURLED ROCKS AT THE ATTACKING FEDERAL SOLDIERS. (LC)

formation along Lewis Lane (the southern extension of the Groveton-Sudley Road) and on a partially wooded ridge to the east. Hood's soldiers, "yelling all the while like madmen," easily brushed aside the six companies holding Lewis Lane and swept forward against Warren's main position.

In a matter of moments the rest of Warren's brigade disintegrated. "The only hope of saving a man was to fly . . . for in three minutes more there would not have been a man standing," reported a participant. The Fifth New York, a proud unit that would produce eight generals from its ranks, suffered more men killed in ten minutes than any other regiment would lose in a single battle during the entire

The men of the Fifth New York tried in vain to halt the Texans of John Bell Hood's brigade.

(NPS illustration by Anthony Ranfon.)

Civil War. A witness compared the aftermath of this fight to a "posy garden," referring to the corpses of the Fifth New York in their gaudy Zoauve uniforms. Hazlett's battery fired as long as it could then departed with remarkable discipline.

Pope and McDowell now began to understand the magnitude and consequence of their mistaken strategic analysis and took immediate steps to salvage the battle and save their army. Orders went out to occupy Henry Hill, undeniably the right move but an endeavor that would consume considerable time. The Ohioans of Nathaniel McLean's brigade with whatever reinforcements Pope could quickly muster would bear the awful responsibility of purchasing that time.

McLean, the distinguished son of a congressman and Supreme Court justice, aligned his four regiments facing west on the narrow open crest of Chinn Ridge, about one-half mile east of where Warren met disaster. A battery of artillery unlimbered in the center of McLean's 1,200 men, who girded themselves to receive Hood's impending assault. "As soon as our retreating troops got out of the way, I opened upon the enemy with my artillery and as they came nearer, with a heavy fire from my infantry," reported McLean. Combined with a barrage launched from Federal guns north of the turnpike, McLean's fusillade "drove them back more rapidly than they had advanced."

Now Hood summoned Evans's troops to recapture the temporarily stalled Confederate momentum. Evans shifted his regiments toward the south and charged up the slope of Chinn Ridge against the Federals' left flank. But McLean responded by redeploying two of his units to the point of danger and Evans receded into a patch of piney woods to regroup. The Union line had held, at least until the next Rebel onslaught.

That threat would come from the dark-uniformed Virginia brigade of Montgomery Corse, a portion of Kemper's division. Corse, a forty-six-year-old banker and former militia officer from nearby Alexandria, wheeled his regiments into line nearly at right angles to Evans, facing north rather than east. As Corse's Confederates approached the Buckeyes, the Ohioans initially mistook them for friends, allowing the Virginians to close the distance without opposition. Soon enough, however, the Unionists corrected their error and unleashed a crashing volley from behind a rail fence near the Chinn house. A soldier in the Seventeenth Virginia reported that the Northern blast "came upon us with the suddeness of a thunderbolt. We all sprang forward with one ringing yell—the officers waving their swords and the men standing still only long enough to fire off their guns." The ensuing battle raged for ten minutes at point-blank range, but when a

"Oh This is a Dreadful War"

Alfred Davenport was a member of the Fifth New York Infantry. On the afternoon of August 30, his regiment would suffer the highest number killed and mortally wounded of any Union regiment during the Second Battle of Manassas. He described the destruction of his unit in a letter to his father on September 3, 1862.

"It was not long before a company of the skirmishers came in on our left all much excited, huddled together in a heap and much scared and said that the enemy were coming in and were right on top of us, on the left flank, but before any orders could be given to change position, the balls began to fly from the woods like hail. It was a continual hiss, snap, whizz and slug.

Private Brady, who used to live opposite us in Newington Avenue, in the wooden house was the first one hit—he stood a few files from me. He fell without saying a word, struck in the body. . . . Only the companies on the left could fire. We commenced, but the Rebels' fire was now murderous, our men falling on all sides.

The order had been given to retreat and save ourselves, every man for himself, but we did not here the order. The recruits began to give way and then the whole regiment, broke and ran for their lives. . . . There was no hope but in flight.

While running down the hill towards the small stream at its foot, I saw the men dropping on all sides, canteens struck and flying to pieces, haversacks cut off, rifles knocked to pieces, it was a perfect hail of bullets. I was expecting to get it every second, but on, on, I went, the balls hissing by my head.

How I escaped I don't know but I thank God for it. There are now only eight or ten two-year men left in our company who were at Fort Schuyler when the regiment was first formed. We had then 101 men in our company and I can hardly expect to survive another such engagement; if we should be unfortunate enough to get into another, it will wipe us out as a thing of the past. Oh this is a dreadful war!"

Davenport survived the war and went on to author the history of his regiment published in 1879. He died in 1899 in his native New York.

—Chris Bryce

Destruction of the Fifth New York by Hood's Texas Brigade. (LC)

Louisiana artillery battery added its voice to Corse's determined attackers, McLean's line at last collapsed. The Ohioans suffered 33 percent casualties but with their blood earned Pope thirty precious minutes to rush reinforcements to Chinn Ridge.

The first of these troops belonged to Zealous B. Tower's brigade of Ricketts's division. Galloping up beside Tower came the Fifth Battery of Maine Light Artillery under George Leppien. "The confusion among the troops on the hill was great," admitted one Unionist. "Officers and men shouting, shells tearing through and exploding, the incessant rattle of muskets, the cries of the wounded—all combined made up a scene that was anything but encouraging." Despite the chaos, most of Tower's units efficiently deployed, facing south toward the Chinn house some 300

THE FIGHT FOR CHINN RIDGE, 4:00 P.M. AUGUST 30, 1862
Shortly after the repulse of Porter's attack, Longstreet ordered his men toward the left and rear of Pope's army. Rushing to Chinn Ridge the Federal brigades of McLean, Tower, and Stiles stalled the Confederates, enabling Pope's army to establish a final line of defense on the slopes of Henry Hill.

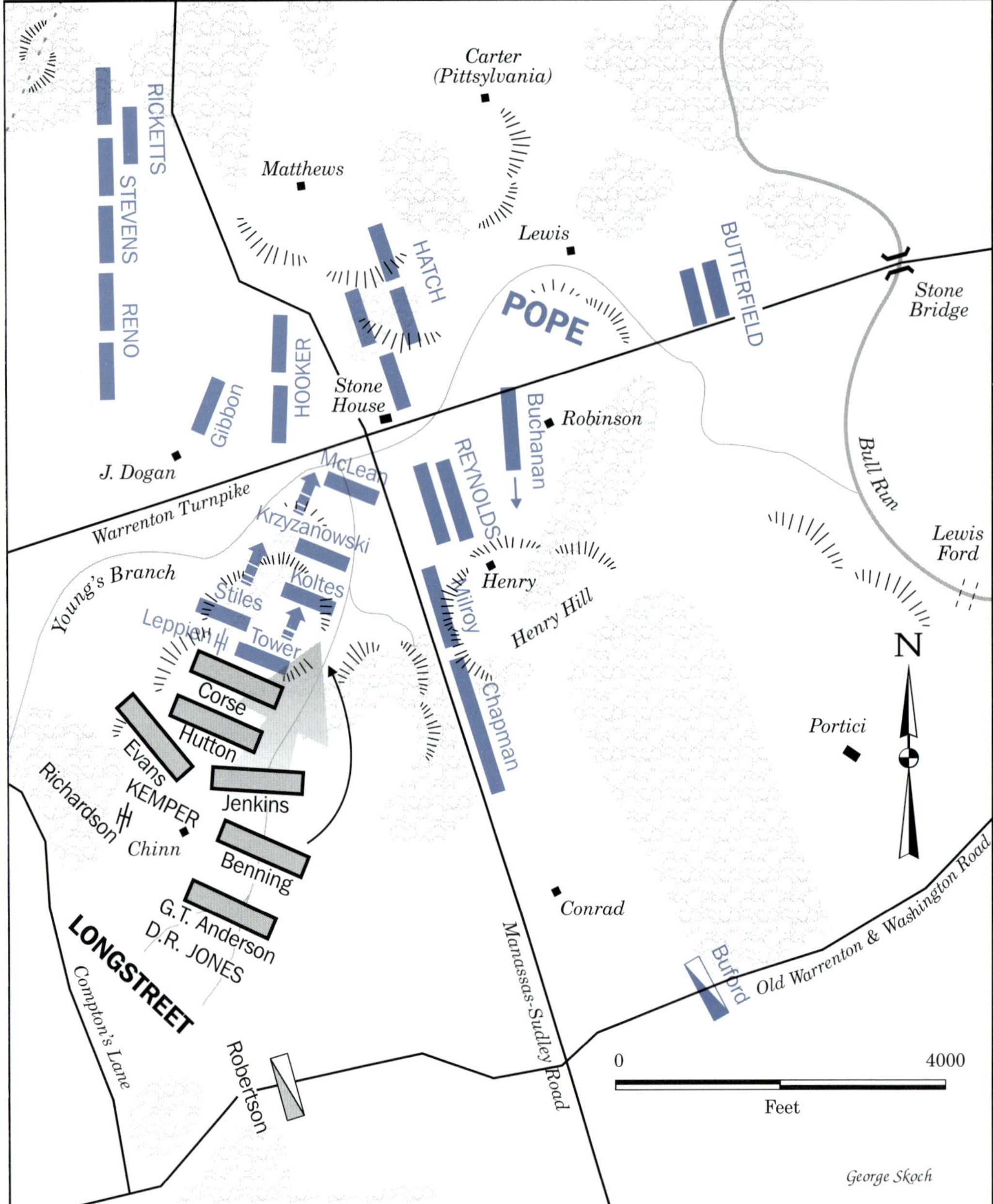

yards away as Leppien's guns roared into action. Now the focus of fighting revolved around Leppien's battery as Hood, Evans, and Corse converged from three sides on the desperate Union resistance. "Nothing could be seen but the flash of the guns," remembered a Confederate as the battle lines melted into a caldron of death in the center of Chinn Ridge.

Some of Corse's regiments had worked their way into the shallow valley of Chinn Branch, east of where Tower and Leppien conducted their defense. Their fire against Tower's unprotected left flank when combined with unrelenting pressure against the Federal right and front eventually determined the outcome. "There was a frenzied struggle in the semi-darkness around the guns, so violent and tempestuous, so mad and brain-reeling that to recall it is like fixing the memory of a horrible blood-curdling dream," remembered a Southerner. But when the smoke cleared, Leppien's battery belonged to the Confederates, Tower had fallen with a serious wound, and a new Union brigade had appeared to play its sacrificial role in the contest for Chinn Ridge.

That brigade belonged to Robert

Stiles and included among its four regiments the Twelfth Massachusetts commanded by Fletcher Webster, son of the celebrated statesman Daniel Webster. "Everything to our hasty glance seemed confusion," confessed one of Stiles's men as the brigade dashed into a rough line behind where Tower had once been positioned. The two other brigades of Kemper's division, Eppa Hunton's and Micah Jenkins's, did nothing to lessen the Federal consternation. They arrived in the Chinn Branch swale and poured fire into the virtually defenseless Federals. "We shot into this mass as fast as we could load until our guns got so hot we had at times to wait for them to cool," reported a South Carolinian. "This mass of Yankees was so near and so thick, every shot took effect."

One of those shots found Fletcher Webster, who tumbled from his horse with wounds in his arm and chest. Webster had written to his wife that very morning explaining that "this may be my last letter, dear love; for I shall not spare myself—God bless and protect you and the dear, darling children." Webster would die within an hour of being hit.

Two more Union brigades arrived on Chinn Ridge, but they experienced even less success than had McLean, Tower, and Stiles. The lead elements of Jones's division, George T. "Tige" Anderson's and Henry L. "Rock" Benning's brigades, at last rendered Chinn Ridge untenable and by 6:00 P.M. Longstreet's troops stood alone in triumph atop the crest. But their final goal still lay several hundred yards away. The ninety-minute Federal defense of Chinn Ridge had measurably weakened the Confederate juggernaut, causing such severe losses in Hood's and Kemper's divisions that they could not participate in the push against Henry Hill. The Fifth Texas alone lost 225 men killed and wounded at Manassas (including a handful who had fallen on the twenty-ninth), more than any other regiment in the army. Darkness would fall in about an hour, and although Lee had clearly won the battle, during the next sixty minutes his best chance to destroy Pope would hang in the balance.

Between 4:00 P.M. and 6:00 P.M. the Union commander did everything possible to prevent such a catastrophe. With commendable energy and reasonable efficiency Pope cobbled together a four-brigade defense line along the western slope of Henry Hill, using Milroy's troops and men

POSTWAR VIEW OF THE CHINN HOUSE, SCENE OF HEAVY FIGHTING ON AUGUST 30.

(LC)

AFTER NINETY MINUTES OF FIGHTING, THE STUBBORN UNION DEFENSE OF CHINN RIDGE CRUMBLED IN THE FACE OF THE ADVANCING CONFEDERATE INFANTRY.

(LC)

"I Shall Not Spare Myself—"

Chinn Ridge, August 30, 1862, the Twelfth Massachusetts Infantry was engaged in the heat of their first substantial battle. Their colonel, brandishing his sword and riding along his line of

FLETCHER WEBSTER (LC)

men, shouted encouragement in an effort to keep them in formation. Suddenly, a bullet pierced his wrist and entered his right breast, causing the colonel to fall from his horse. His adjutant was able to drag the colonel under some bushes nearby. Remaining hidden, they were able to avoid detection by lead elements of the Confederate army. Caught in the maelstrom of battle, their pleas for help went unanswered by Union soldiers engrossed in the fight.

Finally having been discovered by the Confederates, the adjutant begged his captors to take the colonel with them. When they refused, he pleaded to be allowed to remain with the colonel until medical help could arrive. Being denied, the adjutant was forced by the Confederates to leave at gunpoint but was promised that an ambulance would be sent back for the colonel.

Left on the field, the colonel received assistance from several different Confederate soldiers. Knowing that he would soon die, the colonel gave one of these soldiers, Ludwell Hutchison of the Eighth Virginia Infantry, his wallet and asked that it be returned to his family. Hutchison did so after the war had ended.

Two days after the battle, a party was sent out under a flag of truce to retrieve the Union dead and wounded. Among them were two officers of the Twelfth Massachusetts whose purpose it was to locate and retrieve the colonel's body. With the guidance of a Confederate soldier, they found and exhumed the body, discovering that it had been stripped and robbed of a gold watch and over a hundred dollars. The body was sent to Alexandria and embalmed. From there it was sent to the colonel's home and on September 9, 1862, ten days after his death, the colonel was laid to final rest in Marshfield, Massachusetts.

Thus was the fate of Colonel Fletcher Webster, the only surviving son of the famous New England orator and statesman Daniel Webster. He resigned his position as surveyor of the Port of Boston in 1861 to raise and organize the Twelfth Massachusetts. The regiment titled itself the "Webster Regiment" and elected Fletcher as colonel despite his limited military experience.

During his preparation for the coming of his first real battle, Fletcher, in a letter written to his wife on the morning of August 30 stated: "This may be my last letter, dear love; for I shall not spare myself—God bless and protect you and the dear, darling children." His zeal in battle that afternoon proved his letter to be correct.

In 1914 the survivors of the "Webster Regiment" wanted to mark the spot where Colonel Fletcher Webster had died. However, after several failed attempts to locate the site, they sought aid from other sources. Finally, Ludwell Hutchison, upon being contacted, was able to pinpoint the general site of the colonel's demise. Today, a boulder, taken from the Webster family home in Marshfield occupies the solemn locale.

—Terri Bard

from Reynolds's and Sykes's divisions. Two additional brigades provided a reserve, so by the time Longstreet gained control of Chinn Ridge, Pope had established a reinforced line of battle stretching nearly half a mile from the ruins of the Henry house to the south end of the plateau. Pope ordered Banks to sacrifice the army's supplies at Bristoe and move to Centreville, where he could join Franklin, who had at last advanced to the proximity of the battlefield.

Lee realized that Longstreet would need help if he expected to wrest Henry Hill from the stubborn Federals. He therefore dispatched Dick Anderson's three brigades with a portion of Wilcox's division from the Brawner farm about 5:00 P.M, but

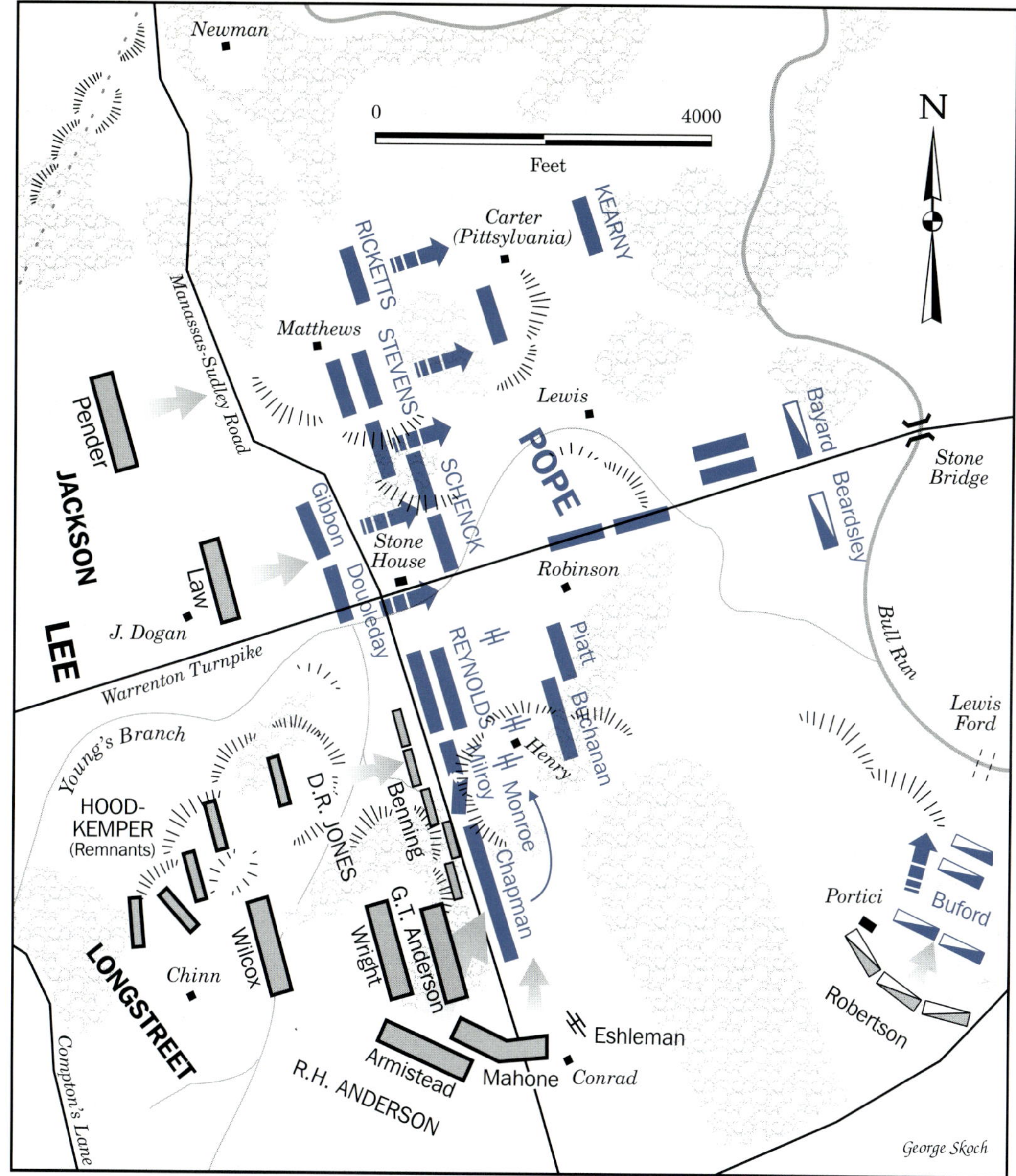

THE CONFEDERATE TIDE CRESTS, 5:00 P.M. AUGUST 30, 1862

After sweeping the Federal troops off of Chinn Ridge, Longstreet's men surged toward the Union line along the Manassas-Sudley Road. Saving the Union army from complete disaster were several Federal brigades stubbornly holding the slopes of Henry Hill. As dusk fell, the Confederate attack was blunted, and Pope's army was able to reach safety across Bull Run.

Anderson would require time to reach the rest of Longstreet's wing on Chinn Ridge. With Hood's and Kemper's commands hors de combat, responsibility for maintaining the pressure devolved upon Neighbor Jones. Jones shifted Benning's and G. T. Anderson's Georgians toward Henry Hill and launched them on another attack.

These 3,000 Confederates represented the largest single assault force of Longstreet's whole offensive. Unfortunately, the Georgians' advance lacked cohesion and discipline. The entire four-brigade Union line punished Jones with a destructive fire that halted the Confederates in their tracks. But just as the Southerners' propulsion seemed spent, William Mahone's and Ambrose R. Wright's brigades of Anderson's division materialized on the Confederate right. The portion of the Union defense line opposite them enjoyed few natural advantages, and the outnumbered Regulars posted there fought tenaciously to hold their ground. McDowell committed his only reserves to the bitter battle on the Union left, but Mahone and Wright outflanked these reinforcements and sent them reeling toward the Henry house. As a result, a Rebel assault from the south could now jeopardize the entire Federal position on Henry Hill and potentially achieve Lee's ultimate goal.

Union soldiers surveying the ruins of the Henry house. (NA)

But Anderson declined to exploit the opening. For reasons that remain unclear, the Confederates held fast on the southern end of Henry Hill. Perhaps the growing darkness intimidated Anderson or the lack of direct guidance from Longstreet and Lee left him hesitant to act. Whatever the cause, Anderson's timidity squandered the opportunity earned by three hours of the most intense fighting of the battle.

North of the turnpike, Stonewall Jackson also failed to apply timely pressure against Pope's reeling legions, but his inactivity is easier to explain. Greatly worn by their three days of incessant fighting and facing, at least initially, the bulk of the Federal army, Jackson's divisions did not begin their portion of the counterattack until 6:00 P.M. But when they did assault, "they came on like demons emerging from the earth." Jackson overran a substantial number of Union artillery and infantry units, but his advance coincided with Pope's orchestrated withdrawal, contributing to the ease with which Jackson achieved his captures. Despite mounting losses, by 7:00 P.M. Pope managed to establish an unbroken line north of the turnpike aligning with the Federal position on Henry Hill. Thus Jackson, like Longstreet, had no choice but to remain content with a substantial tactical victory and the attendant spoils of war while a defeated but intact Union army prepared to leave the field.

Pope issued orders to retreat at 8:00 P.M. as the sounds of battle ebbed away in the darkness. Thanks to its successful defense of Henry Hill, most of the army could use the turnpike and its stone bridge across Bull Run to effect its withdrawal. The gloom of the night and his men's sheer exhaustion extinguished any notion Lee may have nurtured to pursue or harass the Federal flight. By 11:00 P.M. Pope's troops had left the field "with perfect coolness and in good order" and begun to enter the relative safety of the Centreville defenses. Here Franklin's pristine brigades cruelly taunted Pope's veterans as they trudged toward waiting bivoaucs and a well-deserved night's rest.

Robert E. Lee spent the evening contemplating the outcome of the battle. Although he informed President Jefferson Davis in Richmond that "this army achieved today on the Plains of Manassas a signal victory over the combined forces of Genls. McClellan and Pope," Lee knew that his Federal opponents had escaped to fight

The retreating Army of Virginia. (LC)

THE STONE HOUSE NOW STANDS AS A SILENT REMINDER OF THE FIGHTING AT MANASSAS.

(PHOTO BY RAY HELLER)

another day. Should Lee's new strategy succeed, that day would arrive soon.

The gray chieftain resurrected the morning's contingency plan to send Jackson on another flank march around the Union right. Stonewall would depart on August 31, gain the Little River Turnpike, and use that highway to reach the Warrenton Turnpike at Germantown, seven miles east of Centreville and between Pope and Washington. Longstreet would skirmish with the Federals as he had done a week earlier along the Rappahannock, pin them in place, then follow Jackson's route of march. With luck Lee might achieve the knockout blow he failed to land at Manassas. Should the stratagem founder, Lee could safely retreat in several directions.

Pope and Halleck unwittingly played right into Lee's hands. Although on the morning of August 31 Pope's officers voted to retire into the Washington fortifications, a message from Halleck suggested that they stay at Centreville. Pope concurred, thus setting the stage for another one of Stonewall's immortal flanking maneuvers. But Jackson's troops had reached their physical limits. They covered barely ten miles on August 31, encamping at Pleasant Valley Church on the Little River Turnpike.

On September 1 Stonewall resumed his march but quickly encountered Union patrols, erasing the vital element of secrecy from his operation. Jackson decided to halt at mid-morning near an old mansion known as Chantilly and await Longstreet's arrival. Pope had indeed learned of Jackson's approach and dispatched Reno's Corps under Isaac Stevens along with Kearny's division to delay the Confederates while the rest of the Federal army moved back from Centreville to protect the cross-roads at Germantown.

UNDER THE COVER OF DARKNESS, POPE'S DEFEATED ARMY WITHDREW ACROSS BULL RUN TOWARD CENTREVILLE.

(LC)

At noon Jackson resumed his cautious advance, halting two hours later at Ox Hill, where the West Ox Road crossed the Little River Turnpike. Here he deployed to wait for Longstreet and to learn from Lee about the army's next move. But before the Confederates could

THE STONE BRIDGE, OVER WHICH POPE'S ARMY RETREATED ON THE NIGHT OF AUGUST 30.

(LC)

be reunited, Stevens and Kearny crashed into Jackson's lines about 5:00 P.M. amid a violent thunderstorm. During the next two hours a battle ensued that one Confederate characterized as "a beastly, comfortless conflict." Both Stevens and Kearny were killed (no generals died at Second Manassas), but the wild fighting ended indecisively about dark. That night as Pope's army safely drew back toward the capital's elaborate earthworks, Lee recognized that Pope had slipped his noose and that the Second Manassas Campaign had finally concluded.

The Second Battle of Manassas had been one of the most costly engagements of the Civil War. Lee lost 1,300 killed and more than 7,000 wounded during the three days of major fighting, while Pope suffered nearly 10,000 casualties, not counting those captured or missing. In the woods and fields from the Brawner farm to Henry Hill, along the unfinished railroad and on Chinn Ridge, in unnamed hollows and behind shattered trees, the bodies of the fallen littered the landscape. Unburied corpses "who had been dashing and gallant soldiers only a short week before . . . were swollen, blistered, discolored . . . and emitting odors so thick and powerful that it seemed they might have been felt by the naked hand."

Those who survived the battle faced an uncertain future, particularly Union commander John Pope. On September 2 Halleck informed Pope that Lincoln had named McClellan to assume control of the combined armies and ordered Pope to conduct the troops to the Washington

ISAAC STEVENS

(USAMHI)

Encounter at Lewis Ford

The evening of August 30, 1862, saw a struggling Union army preparing to retreat over Bull Run. Reeling from Longstreet's crushing counterattack, the Federals clung tenaciously to the slopes of Henry Hill. Lee saw the chance to strike Pope's route of retreat and administer the final blow to an already battered army. Lee called on the masterful J.E.B. Stuart to administer this maneuver. Promptly, Brigadier General Beverly H. Robertson with Colonel Thomas Rossers's regiment of cavalry were ordered forward. In the hands of these Confederate commanders lay the chance to envelop and destroy the entire Union army.

Having received his orders, Robertson headed for Lewis Ford, south of the Union army's line of retreat. Approaching the ford, Robertson observed a "small squadron" of Union cavalry and ordered the Second Virginia to charge them. Colonel Munford led his command in a race for the enemy and scattered them. However, lurking behind the squadron was General John Buford with his brigade of cavalry. Recognizing each other, the forces charged one another. Numerically superior, the Union cavalry soon had the advantage. Abruptly, the Confederates were reinforced and the tide of battle changed. Federal forces fled toward the retreating army. Having pursued, the Confederates soon found themselves behind the Union army with darkness coming on and so withdrew to a safer position, ending the skirmish.

Although lasting only a few moments, Lewis Ford was a vicious fight. Confederates and Federals went toe-to-toe armed with only sabers and pistols. Horses and riders were thrown together. One participant stated that "the shooting and running, cursing and cutting that followed cannot be understood except by an eyewitness." Caught in this melee, Confederate Colonel Munford was dismounted and severely slashed across his back. Union Colonel Brodhead was shot point-blank after refusing to surrender. Even General Buford, who led the Union cavalry, was wounded in the knee. In a violent, costly, and desperate battle, the Union achieved much from the sacrifices made at Lewis Ford.

Lewis Ford, besides being one of the largest cavalry conflicts up to that time, had two other important repercussions. First, General Buford managed to withstand and delay the enemy long enough to save the Union army. Had Buford not been there and stood up to the Rebels, Pope and his entire army would have been lost. As Buford charged, a new and valuable player entered the war. Union cavalry had never initiated a stand-up fight until this time. From this point on, the cavalry of the Union was going to make its presence on the battlefield known. The encounter at Lewis Ford saved an army and demonstrated how Federal cavalry in the Civil War was beginning to develop.

—Jason Litchblau

defenses. Little Mac cantered out that afternoon and encountered Pope and his staff near the head of the column. When word of McClellan's ascension filtered through the army, cheers echoed up and down the ranks. One can only imagine Pope's thoughts as he rode almost alone toward the Potomac and the practical termination of his Civil War career.

Two other Federal officers saw their reputations ruined at Second Manassas. Although a court of inquiry cleared Irvin McDowell of any wrongdoing, the perception of McDowell's incompetence, disloyalty, and even treason resulted in his banishment to an inconsequential post in California. Fitz John Porter fared even worse. Porter had been the most outspoken of McClellan's officers in his denunciations of Pope, and he cared little about who knew his feelings. Those sentiments added a veneer of credibility to Pope's unfair accusation that Porter caused his defeat at Second Manassas. A court-martial convicted Porter of willfully disobeying Pope's attack orders on August 29, and Porter devoted the next twenty years to restoring his good name.

The Northern populace cringed at the news from Manassas. Not only did the casualty lists bring grief into thousands of homes, but the likelihood of ultimate Union victory seemed dimmer than ever. "To think that we should be conquered by the bare feet and rags of the South," lamented a New York woman. Some

The Northern populace cringed at the news from Manassas. Not only did the casualty lists bring grief into thousands of homes, but the likelihood of ultimate Union victory seemed dimmer than ever.

Federal soldiers also lost faith in the outlook for the war. "We had plenty of troops to whip them," protested Robert Milroy, "but McDowell is a traitor and Pope is an incompetent egotist. . . . Lincoln is blinded and under bad advisors and things will go from bad to worse. I see no hope. Our govt. is lost and we must bequeath war misery and anarchy to our children."

Events certainly appeared brighter for the Army of Northern Virginia and the cause it championed. During a two-month period, Lee had moved the war in the East from the doorstep of Richmond to the outskirts of Washington. But he had paid a terrible human price for this achievement. His weakened army lacked the firepower to fight on anything like equal terms with his Union opponents. Moreover, northern Virginia lay ravaged by military occupation and its prostrate farms could not sustain even Lee's depleted numbers. The Confederate commander could either withdraw south closer to reliable sources of supply or risk a raid across the Potomac into Maryland and Pennsylvania, subsisting his army off the bounty of Northern agriculture. The incomparable Virginian chose the bolder of these two options and on September 4 began the march that would result two weeks later in the Battle of Antietam.

Understood in this context, the Second Manassas Campaign marked the midpoint of Lee's grand summer offensive in 1862—a period that in retropsect would mark the true high tide of Confederate fortunes. Observers in foreign capitals took note of the apparent viability of this new government whose armies could win victories within the shadow of Washington. Voters in the North embraced Democratic candidates for Congress who challenged the management and even advisability of the conflict. And Abraham Lincoln deferred announcing the plan, his preliminary Emancipation Proclamation, that would in the end add transcendent meaning to the carnage of the Civil War.

A PERIOD LITHOGRAPH TITLED *LEE AND HIS GENERALS*. THE CONFEDERATE VICTORY AT SECOND MANASSAS ENABLED LEE TO MOVE HIS ARMY NORTHWARD INTO MARYLAND.

(LC)